300

SCRAPBOOKING
your Faith

Layouts
that
celebrate
your
spiritual beliefs

courtney walsh

Memory Makers Books
Cincinnati, Ohio

www.memorymakersmagazine.com

11 10 09 08 07   5 4 3 2 1

Distributed in Canada by Fraser Direct
100 Armstrong Avenue
Georgetown, ON, Canada L7G 5S4
Tel: (905) 877-4411

Distributed in the U.K. and Europe by David & Charles
Brunel House, Newton Abbot, Devon, TQ12 4PU, England
Tel: (+44) 1626 323200, Fax: (+44) 1626 323319
Email: postmaster@davidandcharles.co.uk

Distributed in Australia by Capricorn Link
P.O. Box 704, S. Windsor, NSW 2756 Australia
Tel: (02) 4577-3555

Editor: Christine Doyle
Designer: Marissa Bowers
Layout Artist: Jeremy Werling
Art Coordinator: Eileen Aber
Production Coordinator: Matthew Wagner
Photographer: Christine Polomsky

fw
F+W PUBLICATIONS, INC.

Library of Congress Cataloging-in-Publication Data
Walsh, Courtney
  Scrapbooking your faith / Courtney Walsh.
    p. cm.
  Includes index.
  ISBN-13: 978-1-59963-002-1 (pbk: alk. paper)
  ISBN-10: 1-59963-002-8 (pbk: alk. paper)
  1. Photograph albums. 2. Photographs--Conservation and restoration. 3. Scrapbooks. 4. Faith in art. I. Title.
TR501.W35 2007
745.593--dc22
          2006039759

ABOUT THE AUTHOR

Although she grew up in the church, Courtney Walsh was never one to dream of a life in the ministry. Instead, her dreams involved a stage in New York City. Thankfully, God steered her in the right direction, landing her the role of her life: the wife of a children's pastor and mother of two. Courtney is a life-long scrapbooker and passionate writer with degrees in both theatre and journalism from Bradley University in Peoria, Illinois. She has written several one-act plays and full-scale musicals alongside her husband Adam, who is a musician and creative powerhouse. Together, they have found themselves smack dab in the middle of their calling: ministering to children in Rockford, Illinois. Courtney has worked as a freelance writer and artist for *Memory Makers Magazine* and books and a number of other scrapbooking publications. She is currently searching God's will for this next season of her life and can be reached at www.courtneywalsh.typepad.com.

Dedication

I would like to dedicate this book to my husband, Adam. I know it sounds cliché, but I'm a really lucky girl. He challenges me to believe in my own creativity by believing in it enough for the both of us. He puts up with my insanity just before deadlines and deals with my stress waaaayyy better than I do!

For all the sacrifices you made to see this dream come true, and for the countless ways in which your creativity inspires me, I dedicate this book to you.

Acknowledgments

I've discovered that writing a book is a very involved process! (Who knew?) And it's also one you simply cannot complete on your own. It takes a whole support system to make it happen, and I just so happen to have the best one in place.

First off, my Lord and Savior, Jesus Christ, who constantly reminds me to trust in Him and lean not on my own understanding. Without Him, there would be no reason…

Adam. You already got the dedication, so I'm only mentioning you here so you don't feel left out. (That's a joke.)

Sophia. Thank you for praying every night that I would find creativity. Just hearing those words made me feel inspired. You inspire me.

Ethan. You are too little to understand what I've been doing for the past few months, but you have been a good boy, and for that I am grateful. Thank you for offering to pray. It worked!

My mom and dad. You taught me about the love of Christ by living out what you believe. I am in awe of you. And so, so grateful for the times you took the kids for the days or overnight. You may not have realized it, but those little trips were work days for me. And I'm so grateful.

My sister and Matty. For pretending to be interested in scrap-booking. Okay, you really don't pretend that at all, do you?

But you do encourage me. And for that, I'm really thankful!

Mindy Rogers. You're a Sanity Preservationist. For getting me out of the house for long walks where I could not think about being stressed out. Thank you for the relief… day after day!

To the eight artists who worked on this book with me: Jodi, Heather, DeB, Brenda-Mae, Amber, Ruth, Nely and Hanni. For your support. Your prayers. Your creativity. You are all amazing and talented women, and I am so blessed you all agreed to be a part of this book! It is far better because of you.

Jodi Amidei. For the push. I wouldn't have done it without you. I owe you!

Christine Doyle. For the patience. Thank you for being so easy to work with and for your support throughout the process. You are amazing.

And to you. Yeah, you! The one holding the book. I don't know that there would've been a reason to write this book if it weren't for you. This book is for you. It is my prayer that God will use it to inspire you. And even if you don't share my faith, I hope you will be able to stretch your creativity by finding ways these ideas will translate to the religion of your choice.

TABLE OF CONTENTS

INTRODUCTION

First Steps. First Words. Graduations. Birthdays.

Of course you'll find these milestone events on the pages of every scrapbooker's albums. Memories strung together in between each milestone. They make up large chunks of our days...but are they what make us who we are?

I was once told who you are is not defined by what you do. I didn't quite understand the point at the time, but I get it now. There's so much more to me than just what I do with my daily life. Laundry and dishes and carpool—those things don't make me who I am. Days pass into weeks into months into years, and the things I do with my days change as quickly as the seasons, but the person I am remains the same.

My spiritual journey. It's more than a road trip with an ending or a vacation with a few highlights here and there. It is what makes me who I am. All tucked away in a sometimes frazzled, sometimes put-together little package is this soul that longs for God. There's a part of me that needs to know Him more—as a Father and a friend. There are lessons I'm learning as my faith is being challenged. There's a legacy to be left in the things I believe about God. There are beliefs I want my kids to know, prayers I want them to know I prayed, inspiring people they may never know, but who can inspire them just the same...through my pages. Blessings I want to record, if for no other reason, than to remind myself that life is really good.

Your spiritual journey may not be something you think about every day. You may not attend church or work there, as I do. But you still have a belief system. You still have more to you than birthday parties and vacations. If, after you are long gone, someone were to pick up the pages in your albums, would they really know you? Would they know the things you believed, the hopes and dreams and desires of your heart? Would they perhaps feel comforted to know that you too struggled to find your voice, struggled with what you believed, struggled to silence the self-doubt in your mind? Would future generations be able to learn from those lessons you're learning? Would they be inspired by the people who surround you?

Everyone believes in something. Everyone has something in them that will inspire others. Every one of us has a whole list of blessings worth noting. Everyone has a story. Even stories that will stop your heart. What's yours? If you don't tell it, no one will.

CHAPTER ONE | I BELIEVE

*Scrapbooking your beliefs
lets future generations
know the real you.*

WHETHER YOU BELIEVE IN THE BIBLE, the Koran, the Torah or none of the above, odds are you still believe in something. Our beliefs make up who we are. Without them, we are simply statistics. What we believe in separates us from the rest of the world. It makes us unique. It sets us apart or links us together. Our beliefs are at the core of who we are.

Scrapbooking your beliefs lets future generations know the real you. They'll even know what you thought about topics not right for mixed company. Religion. Politics. Controversial issues you have every right to include in your albums, even if you rarely talk about them in real life. If you leave this portion of your personality out of your albums, your readers will never know who you really are. And if you're scrapbooking to preserve memories—to preserve the memory of you—it would be a shame to leave future generations with an incomplete picture.

Consider your beliefs. What are they? What do you most want people to know about your belief system? How does it contribute to the person you are?

BUT WHY?
THE BOTTOM LINE:

Because you are more than a wife, a mother, a sister, a friend. No one label can describe everything that you are. Who you are is made up of what you believe. Your character is defined by your beliefs, your personality and the way you interact with others. *So…what do you believe?*

"I AM THE WAY AND THE TRUTH AND THE LIFE NO MAN COMES TO THE FATHER EXCEPT THROUGH ME"

I Believe

Can what we believe be broken down into one main thought? Maybe not. Beliefs are full of twists and turns—conditions and contexts. At the same time, in my faith, the most fundamental, basic belief is that Jesus is the Son of God. That belief in Him is the only way to heaven. Many religions have that one core belief—the one that can't be debated if you are a believer of that faith. It's so important to record that belief. If all of the intricacies of your beliefs are lost somehow, the one big one will remain. This should be the first layout you do: the one that breaks your faith down to a sentence or two.

God hears the tiniest prayers

Ethan always wants to pray. He prays before our meals. He prays before bed. He prays when I have a headache. I love that he prays. But watching him pray reminds me of how God is so faithful to hear even our tiniest prayers... prayers we whisper when we get in a jam. Prayers in the depths of our soul we wouldn't dare say out loud. Prayers most people wouldn't understand. He knows our heart. He knows our desires, our fears. And I know he answers every prayer I pray... the real question is... am I listening?

THE TINIEST PRAYERS

I believe God knows our thoughts. He knows our desires. He wants to come to our side, if only we'd ask. Seeing my son pray reminds me of that. His prayers are often kind of silly and don't always make sense, but he means them. And God gets that. I created this layout to state what we often forget…God is listening. Always ready to hear our prayers. Sometimes a sight like a tiny child praying can come to mean so much. He believes in his prayers. And so do I. As Ethan grows up, I'll keep this layout close by—so he'll always know God is listening.

i believe what i say matters.
i believe in the power of my words.
i believe i can speak life or i can speak death.
it's up to me.

i choose life.

speak life

This layout was directly inspired by a Bible verse we studied in children's church. Isn't it amazing that lessons meant for children can affect us as adults? The verse, James 3:2, says "we all make many mistakes, but those who control their tongues can also control themselves in every other way." What we say matters. The words we speak are important, more so than we realize. I believe there is life and death in the power of the tongue. This layout acts as a profound reminder of that fact.

GOD'S *i believe*

I think I hear
God's heart breaking
As he looks around
and sees what we've
become –
When he sees the hatred
and the sadness
The selfishness,
the suffering
When He calls out
for anyone to answer
And no one is listening
I can hear
God's heart breaking
When we stumble,
when we fall –
In a way that takes
others down with us
Because we've professed
to have the answers.
I think I hear His heart,
breaking in the heavens
When we turn our backs
Refuse to respond to his call
Pretend He doesn't exist
When he is mocked
When we cry
When we suffer.
God's fragile heart is breaking.
We are breaking God's heart.

HEART CAN BREAK

heartbreak

I believe we were created in God's image. Therefore, I believe many of our characteristics come from Him. For a gentle God, I imagine seeing a lot of what's going on in the world is nothing short of heartbreak. I wanted to create a page that spoke to the nature of God. To paint a different picture of Him. To make him more real. I know this layout won't likely change all that's wrong with the world, but it can create an awareness in my own circle of friends and family that we aren't alone— our actions do have consequences. And just like a parent, when we sin, we break our Father's heart.

*What phrases only make sense
to other people in your religion?
Find out what they really mean
and do a page about it. In the
future, no one will have to
wonder what in the world
you were talking about.*

INTO
MY HEART

Sometimes we use terminology, passing it down from generation to generation, but never take the time to figure out what it means. Think about your religion. What phrases do you think a new convert would be confused by? One of those phrases for me was "asking Jesus into your heart." I did this at the age of five, and I don't know if I really understood what that meant. It's one of those phrases we use all the time, but never take the time to translate.

jesUS heaL MY bumps

Molluscum Contagiosum. Yeah, we didn't know what it was either until these pimple type bumps showed up on Sophia's face when she was about two and a half. We took her to the doctor for the diagnosis and then tried all kinds of medicine, including wart remover - even a herpes cream. Nothing worked. This went on for a long time - well over a year - and finally I realized I'd never taken her forward for prayer in church. So I did. And within a couple of weeks, the bumps went away, leaving a few tiny little pits in the side of her chest - reminders of how God had plucked them out at the root.

When the same little bumps showed up on Ethan, I knew exactly what they were. I took him forward for prayer, but nothing happened. I took him forward again and still nothing. And then God told me to have Ethan pray for the bumps himself. It sounded a little crazy, I mean, Ethan was only two... but every time I changed his diaper, I made him repeat after me... "Jesus! Heal my bumps!" He did it with such enthusiasm.

It was a pretty simple prayer, but I believed it - and so did Ethan. Within just a couple of weeks, those bumps literally fell off of Ethan's body. Even this one in the center of his chest which was clearly infected. There is so much power in the name of Jesus... and so much power in our faith and our prayers. No more bumps for the Walsh kids... thank you Lord!

FOCUS on FAITH

What have you witnessed that strengthened your faith? Document it so in a time when your faith isn't quite so strong, you can latch onto what God has already done for you.

JESUS, HEAL MY BUMPS

Sometimes we forget to pray for things like the common cold or allergies. We accept them as part of the plight we must endure. I always looked at these annoying bumps the same way until one day it dawned on me: I could actually pray them away. I am a strong believer in the power of prayer, and I wanted to document what to many would seem like a tiny miracle. It not only builds my faith, but in the future, I am quite sure it will build the faith of my children. Once you see God work in small ways, you start to believe He can tackle the big things for you too.

Life is, of course, full of its ups and downs. Challenges and trials are a part of our daily life. But when we come out on the other side of them, able to stand, and stronger than before, there's a hint of the divine, resting a hand on our shoulder and encouraging us. Don't forget to document these moments—the kinds of moments words alone may never rightfully convey.

SHE SEES ANGELS

{SHE SEES ANGELS

...in the rafters, in the clouds, you can tell by the smile on her face. She's close to heaven, farther from earth— given a gift.

She's a miracle—a reason to believe in god's promises—like a rainbow to all who know her...

And in her smile and in her eyes I can see the angels... and once again I remember why I believe.

EMERY — 6 months

My niece, Emery, is such a special baby. It's like there's a light glowing over her. I believe in angels. I believe God sends them out to protect us and keep us safe. And every once in awhile, in Emery's eyes, you'll see them. It's like they're playing with her, trying to make her laugh. This little baby's life is a reminder that God is our healer. The very fact that she is alive reminds me every day that I need to trust in Him. She reminds me why I believe what I believe.

he doesn't live behind stained glass.

he doesn't wear dressy clothes.

he doesn't only visit on Sundays.

he doesn't.

i might have left my church—

but i didn't leave him.

and he didn't leave me.

anytime i need him, i just look within... and i know he is there.

just LOOK RIGHT HERE &

always HE WILL be there

THROUGH THICK & THIN

JUST LOOK RIGHT HERE *by Amber Clark*

For Amber, her belief in God extends beyond the walls of a church. Having left the idea of organized religion behind, Amber has found God resides much closer to home: right inside her heart. We all have beliefs about God and a higher power. Whether you believe in Him or not, these are still the kinds of thoughts and ideas you owe it to yourself to record. Amber's page is simple in what it says, but it speaks volumes about what she believes. It's real and honest—completely raw. Don't you want your readers to feel they know you that intimately?

IN CHRIST
ALONE

by Hanni Baumgardner

It is through her relationship with Christ that Hanni finds peace, knows joy, is forgiven and has become whole. This layout celebrates these aspects of her Christian walk in a clever and unique way. By attaching her patterned circles to flat magnets, Hanni has created a cover for her journaling blocks. The backs of each magnet are attached to the back of the page. Each circle houses a different one of Hanni's beliefs about her relationship with Christ. Not only is this layout fun, but it's also an important part of Hanni's legacy.

Dear Lord,

I pray for the creativity you have in your little finger..." That's been my prayer for a long time now. I reason that if I had that much creativity, I would have more than anyone on earth. Look around - there is no greater artist than God. From creating weeds disguised as cute yellow flowers to the wide array of animals - many I'll never see... I'm in awe of the innovation and creativity of our Creator. I imagine God in Heaven, still coming up with new faces for our babies... animals that break the mold just a little bit... or a flower more beautiful than any ever seen. I imagine He's the kind of artist who doesn't quit, who never settles... the kind who is always looking for a way to think outside the box. I believe God has created me in His image... and there are so many facets of His character that I hope I have. Of all of the though, for me, being creative has got to be one of the most important. (thoughts from our trip to the Madison Zoo, August, '06)

GOD IS A CREATIVE GENIUS.

FOCUS on FAITH

Which of God's traits do you most admire? Why? Are they ones you possess or maybe ones you know are far from your reach? Do a page in His honor.

creative genius

Because I love just about everything that is creative—arts, music, drama—I think I am drawn to this aspect of God. I realize we are made in His image, so it would make sense that there is a sect of people who are artistic and creative. But none of us can hold a candle to Him. Every time I see the dandelions popping up or catch a cardinal flitting around outside my window, I'm reminded of His. And while I know I can never have that much creativity, I do pray for just a little bit. I believe God is the master artist. The one to emulate. It's from His work that I want to draw my inspiration.

How do you hear God's voice?
How do you know it's God?
What do you believe about
God speaking to us?

It was early in the year 2000 when I really learned how to recognize God's voice. Before that, I always doubted what I was hearing was really Him. After all, I was an actress... I was good at having conversations with myself. But one spring night, I was awakened by this horrible feeling... and a heavy, heavy burden to pray for Adam. Something told me, clear as day... "there will be an attack on his life today."

We'd only been married a few months, and I was terrified. I'd never loved anyone like I loved Adam. The only person I knew would be awake at 5:30 a.m. was my dad, so I called him and told him what I felt. He told me I needed to pray, and I remember him saying, "It's harder now that you really love someone, isn't it?" I knew he understood.

I prayed. For a very long time I prayed. I covered my husband in prayer and then we went to work. Adam was working at the school and I was at the church, but we were meeting for lunch along with two other pastors. We must've miscommunicated because the three of us from the church hopped in the car and headed over to the school. Not long after, Adam hopped in his car, heading to the church. The road was in the country, and the pastor driving was a practical joker. When he saw Adam's car coming at us, he decided it would be funny to swerve into Adam's lane.

I don't think he knew how close to Adam we were because we ran him off the road.

Instantly, my morning came rushing back. I know it could've been a coincidence, but I doubt it. It was such a close call, and it almost went horribly wrong. Since that day, I've never doubted that still, small voice. The one that tells me to take a different way home. The one that tells me when it's time to walk away from a destructive relationship. The one that tells me when I need to pray for someone. I am so thankful I listened.

STILL
small
voice

Over the years, I've learned to hear the voice of God. People laugh, wondering if He calls me on the telephone or messages me on the computer. But God isn't quite so obvious. I really believe God speaks to us in a quiet voice sometimes, wondering if we'll slow down long enough to listen. On this day, I was so relieved I'd prayed. And while I can't say my prayers definitely kept my husband from harm's way, I can say I'm glad I don't have to wonder if my prayers *would've* kept him from harm's way. Sometimes it's best to trust that voice inside... and later, you can thank God for the warning.

On the scrapbook layout:

I know GOD has **A SensE of huMoR**

Because

I can hear him

laughing at me

right now.

Potty training Ethan sits on the toilet, unrolling an entire roll of toilet paper and flushing. Twice. I watch in horror as the water rises and the spills out over the bathroom floor. The **carpeted** bathroom floor. I begin shrieking, throwing towels on the floor, dialing the church like a madwoman. Two secretaries later Adam is telling me to turn off the toilet. You can turn off a toilet? Who knew? I'm calming down. Until I hear the water dripping through the ceiling and into the downstairs (carpeted) bathroom. I want to cry. I get the shop vac. I begin sucking up water. The shop vac is full of dust. The nasty, dusty water begins to spill out of the shop vac and onto the carpet. And that's when I hear it. God must be laughing... because I recently prayed that we could get new flooring in the bathroom. I guess He heard me... and decided to have a little fun.

FOCUS on FAITH

What do you believe about the nature of God? Do you see Him strictly as a disciplinarian, or have you found the softer side just as prevalent? Find time to explore God. You might discover He's not so unlike you.

A sense of humor

I believe God has a sense of humor. Since we're a lot like Him, wouldn't it stand to reason that our ability to laugh comes from *Him*? Sometimes, however, what I think is funny and what *He* thinks is funny are two different things...at least initially. On this day, I really felt like I was on a hidden camera show. It was one thing after another, and there seemed to be no end in sight. Finally, it got so ridiculous, I had to laugh! And when I looked back on it, it was clear that maybe God just wanted to settle me down a minute, to keep me from taking myself so seriously. Next time, I hope I learn the lesson on my own!

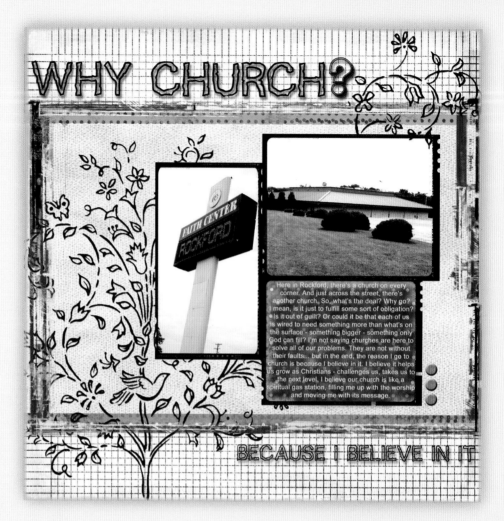

WHY
CHURCH?

I bet you think I have to believe in church…my husband, is after all, employed by one. But the truth is, I would go to church even if we didn't work in a church. I believe in what it stands for. I love the idea of a group of like-minded people gathering together to build each other up. I love that I can go in and get filled up, ready to face another week. I love that even though the pastors don't have all the answers, they have a lot of what I need, and they're willing to give it. When I was a teenager, I didn't see the need for church. I hope to instill in my kids its importance, and this layout is just the beginning of that.

in one God, three divine persons: the Father, the Son, and the Holy Spirit
God created the heaven and the earth, all things seen and unseen
Jesus was conceived by the Holy Spirit and born of the Virgin Mary
Jesus was crucified for our sins. He died and rose again on the third day
everyone has access to forgiveness and eternal life, through Christ
we are saved by faith
God's love is unending, unchanging, and extravagant
God is almighty. He's compassionate. He's worthy of praise
the Bible is the written word of God
in a kind, loving God who loves me as I am
in a Holy God, who wants to purify of my sins
God answers prayers, and sometimes, the answer is "no."
God wants us to love our neighbors as we do ourselves; it;s not always easy
God wants us to laugh, love, enjoy life and each other
in breaking bread; nothing brings people together quite like food does.
to love God is to obey him
God gave me my husband so I can learn of unconditional love
God gave me my children to teach me patience
in fellowship, hanging out with other Christians
God has a sense of humor
we were created to worship Him.

I believe...

FOCUS on FAITH

*What are your
fundamental beliefs?
Consider making a list
of the most important
aspects of your belief
system—those beliefs
that won't change.
The ones that make
up who you are.*

I Believe *by Nely Fok*

We all have a number of beliefs, especially when it comes to our faith. Rather than create a page
for each one, Nely decided to combine several for one comprehensive (and breath-taking) layout.
Listing various beliefs she holds dear to her heart, Nely clearly conveys the important message
of what she believes in regard to her faith. This layout is so cut-and-dried, there's no wondering
where she stands. Her family will always know how she felt, and that is one of the very best reasons
to document your beliefs!

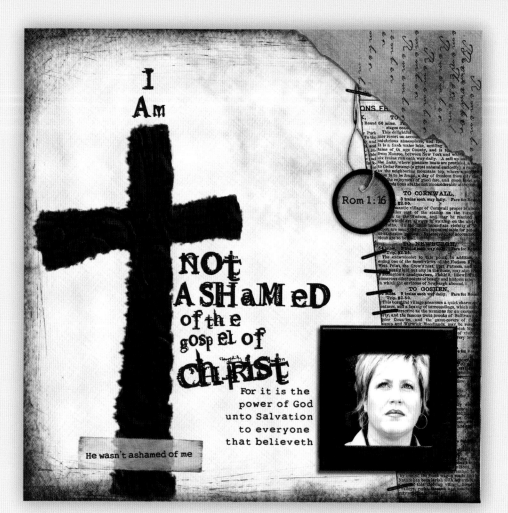

I am not ashamed

by Deb Perry

In this striking layout, Deb makes a bold statement, not only in her design, but in the words she has written. Using just one small photo of herself, Deb lets the sentiment take center stage. For any person of faith, being unashamed of what she believes is important. Perhaps creating a page like this one would serve as the reinforcement you need to be bolder in your faith. Or maybe you, like Deb, are already able to stand up for what you believe. Either way, this sort of layout is more than just words on paper: It's a testimony. A motto. Words to live by. What words will you choose to live by?

faith **kids**

more than just babysitting

At Faith Kids we believe
babysitting is for nights on
the town. We believe your child
should be taught and nurtured,
challenged and loved. We believe
there's something special in each
child that walks through the door
and we believe it's our job to
find it. We believe in having fun,
experiencing God and speaking
life into our kids. At Faith Kids,
we believe there's no one quite like
your child. So if you're looking for a
babysitter... don't call us.

FAITH KIDS

Whether you volunteer for or run a ministry, you are probably passionate about it. I know I am.
I believe in what our ministry stands for, and I am just as passionate about what our ministry does
not stand for. We do not believe in babysitting children. We believe in teaching them. Inspiring
them. Building them up. This layout is almost like a mission statement for me. It reminds me
why I do this. Every day isn't easy. Most days aren't easy…but nothing worthwhile is ever easy.
This layout reminds me that these kids are more than worthwhile.

CHAPTER TWO | # prayers and meditations

A written record of your thoughts and prayers… is a wonderful way to solidify your faith.

I PRAY. A LOT. I HAVE TO—I'm a mom. There are so many different kinds of prayers and so many different ways to pray, but most humans, in one way or another, spend time in prayer. Sometimes through gritted teeth. Other times, through nervous laughter. Long thought-out prayers, or short, under-the-breath prayers... it really doesn't matter. The result is always the same. Prayer is our instant connection to God. It leads us into His presence and gives us a chance to tell Him how we feel, to thank Him for His blessings and to ask Him for what we need.

A written record of your thoughts and prayers, the things you are believing for and expecting God to do, is a wonderful way to solidify your faith. In putting your prayers in writing, you are making a statement that you expect something from God. You expect to be heard. By allowing those you love to become a part of your prayer life through your albums, your family will never wonder what your hopes and dreams were for them. With your prayers in writing, you'll be able to look back on what God has done with gratitude, and that proof of how He has been at work in your life will undoubtedly strengthen your faith.

BUT WHY?
THE BOTTOM LINE:

Scrapbooking can be empowering.
By recording our revelations, we
ensure that they won't be forgotten.
We also give ourselves a better chance
to achieve what's been set before us.

Consider an album full of revelations.
Thoughts and ideas on God and
the promises He has for you.
Recording them is a powerful way to
insist that they come to pass.

When you call on Jesus

all things are possible

you cAn mount oN winGs like Eagles and SoaR

When you call on Jesus
Mountains are gonna fall
'cause He'll move Heaven and earth
to come rescue you when you call.
* nicole C. Mullen

WHEN YOU CALL ON JESUS

by Deb Perry

After Hurricane Katrina, Deb began to meditate on this verse, and on the very nature of Christ. Knowing that through Him all things are possible, she created this layout to express what she and many others were feeling at that time. With an entire nation on its knees, Deb wasn't alone in this prayer. How powerful to have a layout to reflect the prayers of her heart during a time she will never forget. Deb's enlarged photo serves as the background for this layout. Don't be afraid to go extra large and embellish directly on the photo. The results are dramatic!

Looking around at nature, we can reflect on many facets of God's personality. What do the flowers or the trees make you think of? How much closer to Him do you feel when you have His handiwork in your sight?

THE LITTLE THINGS

I am always amazed at how detail-oriented God is. He literally thinks of everything. It's obvious just looking at nature, or the human body. He has remembered the very tiniest things. I created this layout to really celebrate the nature of God. A God who doesn't leave anything out. A God who decorates the trees with little tiny dots of color. A God who even makes the weeds pretty to look at. I want that aspect of God's character. I want everything I touch to be more beautiful because I've touched it.

*Sometimes talking with
teenagers about God proves
a difficult task. Why not
write it down instead?*

BLESSING
LINDSAE

by Deb Perry

Certain prayers stick with us for years, as is the case with Deb's blessing for her children. This layout, which she made to display on the wall in her daughter's room, will ensure that Lindsae knows, even though she's not a little girl anymore, the sentiment and the prayer is still the same. A layout like this one is the perfect way to share your desires with an older child who may not realize they are still an important part of your prayers. They may be old enough to pray on their own, but that doesn't mean our prayers stop.

I pray you continue to watch over us... keep us safe and protect us... keep us in the shadow of your wings. Thank you for your awesome glory - you are holy in every way. I magnify you with the praises of my heart, it's what you've created me to do. And as a father provides for his child, so do you provide for me - so do you love me and keep me safe. Lord, please take control of my life. I am in your hands - as clay - as putty on a potter's wheel. Mold me into the shape you desire. Make me into the person you want me to be. Lord, I pray only your will be done in my life. Teach me to serve you - with my whole heart - to love you with my soul... from the core of my being. I am forever yours.

I pray

Ever since my house got louder (with the addition of two children) I've been writing my prayers down. It's easier to keep my mind from wandering if I'm writing. Some of my prayers are very specific to things I'm going through at the time. Others, however, are prayers I could pray every day of my life. This is one of those prayers. Prayer journals are common among religious people, but I want my journals to reflect more of me. I love to include photos and use my scrapbooking to celebrate who God is, to give my life over to Him, to pray the prayers I need to pray.

So do not
FEAR
for I am with you;
Do not be dismayed
FOR I AM YOUR GOD.
I will strengthen you
and help you;
I will uphold you with my
righteous RIGHT HAND.

fear not
fear not
FEAR NOT
FEAR NOT

Ever since 9-11, I have found myself fearing things I never would've feared before. For instance, the nuclear power plant that is practically in our back yard. I really never gave it a second thought growing up, but when I started paying attention to the news... and power plants were noted as potential targets. I really allowed it to sort of haunt me. I mean, this is the site only 10 minutes from our house... a tiny little town just happens to be home to this huge potential threat to our nation's security. For the past five years, I've been afraid of what might happen. I've allowed the fear - at times - to grip me. I've allowed it to consume me. And there's nothing that gives me comfort... until I turn to the Word of God. Over and over again, God commands us not to fear. He gives us the comfort I so often need, reassuring us, encouraging us... making it crystal clear that He will never leave us or forsake us. Without this reassurance, I think by now, I would've had to have been committed somewhere. I struggle with worry and fear and anxiety in such a real way - it's so incredibly tangible to me - and that scares me... but I know, every time I open my Bible - every time I start to fear, he brings to remembrance His promises. Promises that I know I can trust. Promises I am thankful to rely on. Promises I cling to in my darkest hours.

Fear NOT

I created this layout as a way to meditate on a verse I know I need to get in my head and in my heart. With wars, terror and natural disasters in our world today, it's hard to stay focused on Him and what the Bible says: I should not be afraid. I wanted to create a page that helped me get over my inability to trust, the struggle to rest in Him, knowing my life is in His hands. In addition, I've created a layout that is real and honest—exploring feelings I may not often verbalize. Isn't it easier sometimes to write about the way you're feeling, rather than talk about it? Another reason to record your thoughts in your scrapbooks!

INVISIBLE *by Brenda-Mae Teo*

Sometimes we need to create an outward expression of an inward feeling. Just getting it out there makes us feel better somehow and gives us the strength to move on. For Brenda-Mae, this layout was a way to deal with her disillusionment about the way certain things happen in the world. Frustrated with her own inability to discern good and bad, Brenda-Mae found herself running back to God for the comfort and support she needed. The resulting layout is a reminder that He is in control of all things, even when it seems He is silent. The poem was given to her during this time of searching by her sister-in-law, Johanna Ong. What a wonderful complement to a page about this important revelation!

for you are our **father**, who loves and cares for us ∗ for you are our **creator**, who knows our hearts and minds ∗ for you are our **counselor**, who knows the way and is the way ∗ for you are our **provider**, who knows our every need ∗ for you are our **king**, sovereign over our lives ∗ for you are **faithful**, no matter how great our doubts ∗ for you are the **giver of peace**, peace beyond our understanding.

love

praise you, Lord

by Nely Fok

God is always worthy of our prayers, even—no, especially—in times of struggle. For Nely, this page seals that notion, giving her strength and reminding her to praise God, even when our circumstances seem impossible. With her husband's job at risk, Nely began to pray for provision when she felt the Lord telling her to focus on Him and not on the situation. Taking those words to heart, Nely created this layout as a way to keep its importance in the forefront of her mind. Praise Him...even in the midst of adversity.

Because God's your refuge, the High God your very own home, Evil can't get close to you, harm can't get through the door. He ordered his angels to guard you wherever you go. If you stumble, they'll catch you; their job is to keep you from falling. You'll walk unharmed among lions and snakes, and kick young lions and serpents from the path. "If you'll hold on to me for dear life," says God, "I'll get you out of any trouble. I'll give you the best of care if you'll only get to know and trust me. Call me and I'll answer, be at your side in bad times; I'll rescue you, then throw you a party. I'll give you a long life, give you a long drink of salvation!" - Psalm 91:9-16

VICTORY! @ a time.

REFUGE

Do you know someone who is going through a difficult time? Odds are, if you don't right now, you will. My friend Michele handles every battle with an unmatched grace and positivity. Still, I wanted to create this layout for her in case she grows weary. Using one of my favorite uplifting verses and a photo of Michele with her son, a boy whose life is literally a miracle, I hope I've created something she can hold onto, even in the darkest nights. Use your scrapbooking talents to give gifts of encouragement. There's nothing like inspiring someone else or lifting them up by doing something you love to do. They will undoubtedly be blessed for it.

this is where my daughter sleeps. i pray if is a place of peace. may your hand of protection be upon her. may she live out the meaning of her name & have wisdom & excellent virtue. i ask you to protect her innocence. Allow the gifts you've given her to rise so we may know how to encourage her. may her steps always be ordered of you. i thank you for the plan & purpose you have for her & claim them for her life. i pray Sophia would believe in herself & that she would always feel Loved & secure. thank you for blessing us with this amazing CHILD.

dear heavenly father...

in Jesus' Name...Amen.

in Jesus' Name...Amen.

a mother's prayer...

A MOTHER'S PRAYER

I pray for my kids all the time. I am always shouting something up toward the heavens, usually in the form of a question like, *"Why* won't they listen to me, God?" or "How can I make them stop playing in the toilet?" I want my kids to hear my prayers echoing in their heads when they come to a point in their lives when they think they can't do something, that they aren't good enough or smart enough or strong enough. In those times, I pray it is my prayers that they latch onto. I created this page to hang in my daughter's room. It is my gift to her, ensuring that no matter what, she'll always know what I asked of the Lord on her behalf.

Lord are you there, do you hear my prayer? Even at 2, you know he's there. You don't need Proof. I was taught as a little girl; and so were you, He hears your prayer. In Heaven. Don't ever forget that just as you need him He needs to hear from you. No matter your age. cut vocabulary or your knowledge He loves you. The child's prayer is yours.

CHILDS a PRAYER

A CHILD'S prayer *by Ruth Akers*

There are few things more touching than the prayer of a child. Prayers from the most innocent heart, prayed from the purest of people. Ruth's layout is an encouragement to her daughter to continue praying—a reminder that no matter how young she is, God still hears her. Through this page, Ruth has placed importance on her child's prayers, reinforcing a lesson on the topic her daughter won't likely forget.

IN THIS STORM

by Ruth Akers

Living in this day and age, many rely on God for peace of mind. Ruth's poignant page is a reflection on the more disturbing current events headlining the news today. Her page makes the important point that no matter what is going on in the world, she will still praise God through it all. Using a newspaper clipping, Ruth is able to reinforce the "news" theme of her layout. Sometimes our layouts are ones we need to create—to remind ourselves to tune out what's going on in the world and focus on Him.

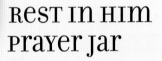

REST IN HIM prayer jar

by Hanni Baumgardner

Hanni's prayer jar is more than just something pretty to look at. It is also a visual reminder to cast her cares on God. By writing her prayers down on a slip of paper and putting them into this jar, she is able to relinquish control of them, truly giving them over to God. As the jar fills up, Hanni can look through her requests, able to see beyond a shadow of a doubt that God truly does answer prayers. Consider making a prayer jar with your children or maybe giving them as gifts to those you love. What a wonderful way to remind someone to rest in God, to give their cares over to Him.

lamentations *by Brenda-Mae Teo*

Every once in awhile, a verse will touch our hearts in a way that is so profound, we know we want to cling to it forever. That was the case for Brenda-Mae with this passage in Lamentations. Rather than let it go unnoticed, she decided to create this piece that she can display, allowing her to always remember the importance of the words. The Bible is an excellent source of comfort. Next time a verse speaks to you, highlight it in a unique way as Brenda-Mae has done here. Give yourself a way to never forget it.

YOU MAKE GOD SMILE

I often relate my own parenting experiences to those God must have with us every day. Nodding when we get a revelation He's been trying to teach us. Frowning when we do something we know we aren't supposed to do. And smiling when we do something silly, like running around splashing in rain puddles. I love that my daughter has a free spirit only a child can possess. I created this wall hanging for her room, showcasing a sentiment that I wanted her to understand: She makes God smile. I want God to be personal to my kids, to know that He's watching her and smiling down on her.

You set me
free to be the
person you created
me to be — you
healed my heart
and made it
whole again — you
are my
everything.

"MY beloved is mine and I am his" ~Song of Solomon 2:16~

BELOVED

by Heather Preckel

The belief that God loves her is a staple in Heather's faith. This verse spoke to her in the early days of becoming a Christian, and she wanted to document its importance. She used the verse as the title and subtitle, and added a personal touch through her own journaling, a prayer to the One who created her. Consider using a verse or meditation that has spoken to you to create a layout you will undoubtedly treasure for years to come.

this is me...at my most transparent.
completely, horribly RAW. No one sees
me like this...blonde eyelashes & all.
But this year, i turned 30-and
it hit me. i am more comfortable
in my skin than i have ever been.
Unashamed of this person. Created
in God's image. Fully aware that by
His standards, i will always be more
than enough. Suddenly, Raw isn't quite
so scary.

totally **raw**

utterly **RAW**

painfully **raw**

Raw

Like most women, I often struggle with insecurities…about how I look or what I'm wearing or
my parenting skills. We all doubt ourselves. This layout is very personal to me, first of all because
there's a photo of me completely raw. But I wanted to scrap it because this is how God created me.
I needed to remind myself that the Word says I am fearfully and wonderfully made…even without
mascara. This layout is a prayer of thanks, but it's also a declaration—that I am OK just how I am.
Now that I have it in print, I hope I never forget it.

Can you allow for human-fallible mistakes...? Can you Accept me - a pastor's wife - and know that HE died for my sins too!

CHAPTER THREE | # PEOPLE WHO INSPIRE

At the heart of any religion are people. Each with stories to stop your heart.

...willing for a prop...

...wanted you to be your...

...oneself - lots of shouting...

...about - but you were the...

...You were very...behaved...

...sensitive to the situation. You...

...that you wanted our friend to get...

...that I told you that we should pray for...

...and that Jesus would make him well...

...We were amazed at your sensitivity and...

...willingness to express the compassion that...

...within you. We are so privileged to...

...and witnesses of God's work in your life.

...see the that the Spirit can work...

...littlest of persons and that...

...enlarged my faith.

YOU made me

SP

MY LIFE IS FILLED WITH amazing PEOPLE. People who inspire me to do what I don't think I can do. People I admire for making the right choice in a tough situation. People who have lived lives I have only lived on a movie screen. There is a wonderful collage of people whose faith helps me maintain my own walk. Knowing them challenges me to live out what I believe. God has put these people in my life for a reason, because He knows they will bless me in ways I have yet to realize.

I love scrapbooking these unique stories that have touched my heart. I love paying tribute to a pastor, a leader, a child or a friend who has changed my life for the better. I love taking those small deeds that someone may have thought went unnoticed and bringing them into the light. I love the way my faith has brought me the best friends of my life. At the heart of any religion are people. Without them, the religion dies. So many stories to stop your heart. Scrap them. If you don't write them down, who will?

BUT WHY?
THE BOTTOM LINE:

I can't think of a better reason to scrapbook than to highlight the good things in another person. Inspiring people are everywhere. Their stories are powerful. Retell them again and again. Chances are, if they've inspired you...*they'll inspire someone else too!*

your passion

Even if they weren't my relatives, I would value Matt's and Carrie's opinions. They are younger than me, but wise beyond their years. They are passionate in a way I've never been. It is the kind of passion that inspires me to seek God in a new way—to discover Him for myself. I admire traits in others that I don't possess, and that passion is often something I struggle to find. Because their relationship with me has been so instrumental in my own Christian walk, I knew a layout about these two was a must for a compilation of people who inspire me.

I believe there is a difference between talent and anointing. There are many talented people. In their own right. Either they have a gift or they've worked to become amazing at what they do. That's admirable. But there's other people who take that talent and give it over to God. They ask him to bless it. They ask him to use them. They ask him to anoint them. And he does.

Corey Pelley is our worship leader at the church. He's one of the most anointed musicians we know. It's in his lyrics that people find themselves able to convey to God the very cry of their heart. He helps people worship. And while he could be very good on his own, he's amazing having given his gift to God.

Anointed.
As if by divine appointment. Give me anointing over talent any day.

ANOINTED
a ·noint ·ed: (v.) To choose by or as if by divine intervention

Do you know someone who could easily top the charts in the world, but who chooses to use their gifts for the Lord? What an admirable trait, and one that will likely inspire you to do the same!

GOD'S GIFTS

I know a lot of talented people. But when it comes to people who are anointed, the numbers begin to dwindle a bit. Anointing is so different than talent. It's when God takes your talent and slaps his seal of approval on it. I created this layout about the worship leader at our church, a gifted musician and songwriter, because I wanted to highlight the difference between talent and anointing. Corey is anointed in a way that few people could dream of, and I admire his gifts. More importantly, I admire that he is an example of what can happen when you give your gifts over to God—you get a double helping of anointing.

I created this layout in PhotoShop Elements first, printing the entire block of photos out as one solid photo. This made it quick and easy compared to cutting it all by hand. Consider adding journaling strips directly on your photos. Sometimes an untraditional journaling block is the best addition to your design.

ADVOCATE

Our job is still so new to us. We're still learning and discovering the ins and outs of running a children's ministry at a church. But one thing we've already gotten down is that we love these kids. God has been very clear in my directive: Be an advocate for these kids. These kids make me want to do the job He has given me because they are so worth it. How do the people around you inspire you to do more in your job or in your volunteer work? How have you impacted the people around you? These people play a huge role in your story. And these children play a huge role in mine.

Show your true colors.

BOLD

Sarah is one amazing kid. She understands how to worship God & when she does it on stage, people take notice. It's so easy to see the anointing on her & I know God is going to use her mightily. I am so honored to be a part of her life. april '04

this girl is...

anointed.

ANOINTED

It's amazing that a nine-year-old girl can make you want to be a better person and a better Christian. I had the opportunity to work with Sarah when I put together a dance for a children's event at our church. Sarah was instantly a stand-out—her anointing was evident. This little girl inspires me. Her passion for Christ makes me want to follow hard after Him—discover Him all over again. Is there a child in your life whose faith is so big and unshakable they make you want to change for the better? Children are far more in tune than we give them credit for. All we have to do is watch them to find that out.

Keilah: Mommy, you want me to make you a sandwich?

Me: No, thank you.

Keilah: How come? You're not hungry?

Me: No, mommy's fasting today.

Keilah: Did you decide it yourself or did God tell it to you?

Me: I chose to.

Keilah: Sometimes, God tells me things in my heart. But I have to *be quiet first*

Me: What does he say?

Keilah: Different things, like to not be mean to my sister and to pray for people.

How humbling your faith is. Constantly, you remind me about what it is I need to be doing. To be quiet before God. To listen, instead of just yammering at him. To hear His will instead of telling him mine and hoping he'll concede his. To be still. You help me realize just how easily I can get distracted. By daily chores. By the internet. By the world around us. My focus shifts so easily. And I can become off-course without me being the wiser. Thank you for reminding me to be quiet...

Even more humbling is that I had no idea you knew about God speaking to your heart. Your dad and I thought it was too abstract a concept for a five-year-old to grasp so we've never spoken about it with you. Yet, you've already experienced it and recognize it for what it is. I thank the Holy Spirit for teaching you in His time. And I thank you for listening.

BE QUIET FIRST

by Nely Fok

"I love documenting the things my children say," Nely says, "A lot of them are silly, but some are profound." After a conversation with her daughter, Nely found herself inspired by the little girl's perspective. "I want to always remember what she said here," she says, "to be quiet first so I can hear what God is saying to me." She created this layout to remind herself of the conversation and the lesson she learned that day. Don't hesitate to record those moments. Sometimes what seems like the smallest, most forgettable thing is really the moment that will change your life.

I've known Melody was an incredible person for a couple of years now, but it was almost like she wasn't real to me until just a few months ago. It was then that I really had a chance to talk with her one on one - to discover the faith behind the myth that is Melody Ross. Going through her own personal hell, Melody still maintains a grace and a beauty you don't often see. She is still focused on pleasing her Heavenly Father - still seeking His plan and His will - when most people would've turned their backs long ago. And through her pain, she still motivates others to share their stories - to live out their faith. And as she clings to her own faith - and to everything she knows is true, I am in awe of her strength and her beauty. So lucky to call her my friend.

Inspired by you

INSPIRED BY YOU

Melody Ross is the founder and CEO of Chatterbox Inc. The story of her business is inspiring, but for me, there was something about her that was much more important to note. And that is her faith. I recently had the chance to sit down and soak in some of her wisdom. It was amazing to me that in the face of her own storm, she was still encouraging me, inspiring me. I want to be like that. I don't want my troubles to define me. I admire a lot of things about Melody, but this, to me, is the most important. And if it's important, then it deserves a place in your albums.

"Mommy, when will we be done with lunch, I've got to GO!" exclaimed a very antsy Paige.

"Why the hurry? my sister in law questioned.

"I want to go show Aleta my feet!" she answered while dancing all over the kitchen.

Her mom knew exactly what she was referring to. Earlier that morning in church Robin had shared a special Bible verse with the Preschool Sunday School class. "How Lovely are the Feet of those that bring Good News" Rom 10:15b

Apparently, Paige couldn't wait to share the Good News of Jesus with her friend across the street. Afterwards, her Mom watched as she ran all the way home... her feet aglow!

"for how can they hear unless somebody tells them?" Rom 10:15a

April 2006

BEAUTIFUL FEET

by Deb Perry

Children often take our words *very* literally. Having learned a new lesson in Sunday school, Deb's niece not only felt that her feet were beautiful, but she had an itching to share the love of Christ with her neighbors. The excitement of a young child as she learns about Christ is often the push we need to find a new passion in our own Christian walk! When that happens, it's important to record your thoughts…odds are someday you'll find yourself feeling un-passionate again, and having these kinds of inspiring thoughts to turn to could be just the spark you need!

TALENT

GREAT THINGS

gifts

GENUINE

heart

U Just mEan it

U JUST MEAN IT

I love that I am married to a man who means what he says. I love that there's nothing pretentious or fake about him. His sincerity in his worship is a constant inspiration—because he just doesn't care who is around. When it's time to worship, that's what he does. Being more self-conscious, I struggle with that a little bit.

We brought you with us on a hospital visit yesterday. I had expected you to be your usual lively (3-year old) self - lots of shouting, jumping and running about - but you were the complete opposite. You were very well-behaved and incredibly sensitive to the situation. You kept saying that you wanted our friend to get better. When I told you that we should pray for him, you said that Jesus would make him well again. We were amazed at your sensitivity and the willingness to express the compassion that was present within you. We are so privileged to be first-hand witnesses of God's work in your life. You made me see the that the Spirit can work through even the littlest of persons and that alone has encouraged and enlarged my faith.

you made me see

by Brenda-Mae Teo

Just because a person is small, doesn't mean their faith is. Inspired by her son's sensitivity and openness, Brenda-Mae created a page that will help her always remember this very special day. It's a treat to see God working through our children, but sometimes when He does, it affects us even more than it does them. We are taken back to our earliest revelations, discovering God all over again through the perspectives of our little ones. Sometimes it's a question or an observation—but children offer a unique perspective adults often fail to see. The inspiration we can gain from them is priceless.

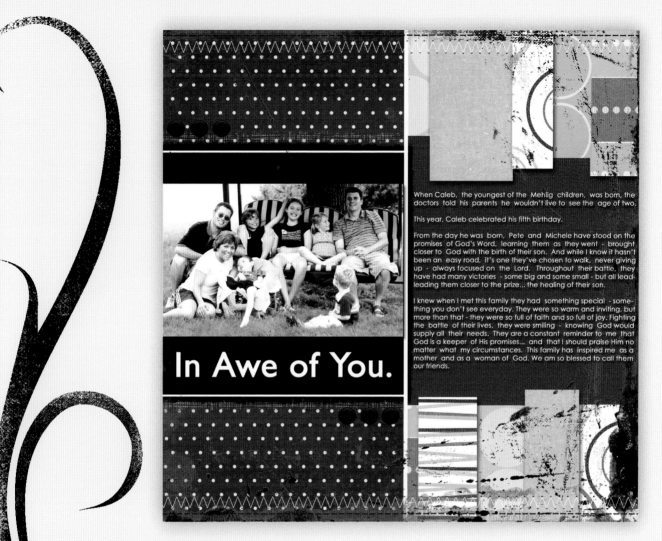

When Caleb, the youngest of the Mehlig children, was born, the doctors told his parents he wouldn't live to see the age of two.

This year, Caleb celebrated his fifth birthday.

From the day he was born, Pete and Michele have stood on the promises of God's Word, learning them as they went - brought closer to God with the birth of their son. And while I know it hasn't been an easy road, it's one they've chosen to walk, never giving up - always focused on the Lord. Throughout their battle, they have had many victories - some big and some small - but all lead-leading them closer to the prize... the healing of their son.

I knew when I met this family they had something special - something you don't see everyday. They were so warm and inviting, but more than that - they were so full of faith and so full of joy. Fighting the battle of their lives, they were smiling - knowing God would supply all their needs. They are a constant reminder to me that God is a keeper of His promises... and that I should praise Him no matter what my circumstances. This family has inspired me as a mother and as a woman of God. We am so blessed to call them our friends.

In Awe of You.

IN AWE OF YOU

Every once in awhile, I'll meet someone—or even a family of someones—who I just know are in our lives for a reason. That was the case with the Mehlig family. The moment we met them, we knew there was something in them that we needed to be around: Extreme Faith. That's what I call it. You assume that people doubt or question or grow weary, but not this family. I am so inspired by the glow surrounding them. The way they interact with each other. The way they fight for their youngest son's complete healing. They make me want to be a better person. They are a gift, and I never want to forget the things I'm learning from them.

Is there a leader in your church who mentors you? Create a layout to show what you've learned from them. Consider giving them a mini album as a thank you.

DELIVERED INTO DESTINY

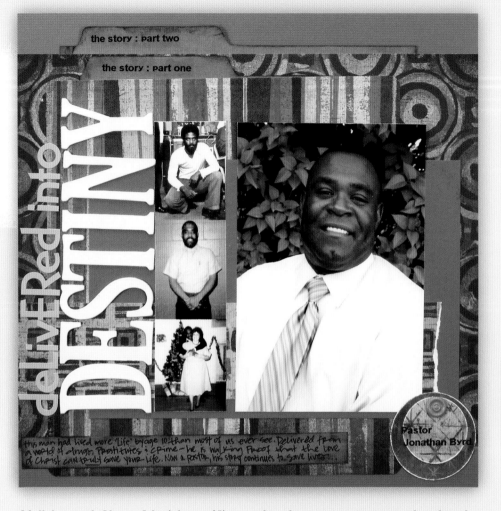

the story : part two

the story : part one

DELIVERED into DESTINY

this man had lived more "life" by age 10 than most of us ever see. Delivered from a world of drugs, prostitutes & crime - he is walking proof that the love of Christ can truly save your life. Now a pastor, his story continues to save lives.

Pastor Jonathan Byrd

Of all the people I know, I don't know if I've ever heard a more inspiring story than that of Pastor Jonathan Byrd. His is a true story of redemption. The moment I heard his testimony, I knew I wanted to remember it. I wanted to document the many times God had reached in and saved this man's life (literally). I wanted to always have the reminder that if God can do that for Pastor Byrd, he can do it for me. We all have people in our lives who have overcome amazing odds. These stories can get us through our darkest hours all the while paying tribute to those who have changed their destiny.

the story : part two

The real trouble for Jonathan came when he got into a fight with a man over drugs. The man pulled a gun – and at the prodding of his friends, was obviously prepared to pull the trigger. Pastor Byrd told me he froze and at the side of his face, he could hear the sound of flesh on the trigger, and in that moment, he knew he wouldn't likely survive. But that's when God intervened. In the life of a man who had really done some terrible things. In the life of a man who didn't deserve it – with a past that would make perfect material for any Hollywood film.

The man pulled the trigger. But the gun didn't go off. Twice. In that moment, Jonathan was able to take a knife and stab the man in the stomach. It sounds terrible, but how many times can a gun NOT go off? What else was he supposed to do? He was able to get away… but soon found himself in prison for murder.

It was in prison that Jonathan hit rock bottom and tried to kill himself. Again, that didn't work. God really wanted this man. I know why. It's obvious. When you listen to his story – when you hear how God used two bickering lawyers to get him a greatly reduced sentence – when you hear how God protected him throughout the nine years he spent inside – you can't NOT believe in God. You can't continue to believe that we serve a God who doesn't care about his children. You can't believe that you have to be perfect before God can use you… if that were true, God would still be waiting…

Since his release from pri[son] ... [off] of our church. He is as solid as they come. Full of knowledge – both biblic... kinds of people. Through his story, you can learn about God's love and g... I love that his heart is t... [Pastor] Byrd my friend. I love that he prays for me.

If you met Pastor Byrd... er know he'd ever been anything *other* th... to live that life so that he would be more... always makes me go back and look for th...

Thank you, Pastor By[rd] ... mansion to be right next to yours.

the story : part one

"How's my friend?" I hear from behind me as I walk into the church. I turn to see this man standing behind me… a man who has, in so many ways, become just that – a friend – to me. You would never know that someone like me (an upper-middle class white girl from small town, Illinois) could actually have anything in common with someone like him (a formerly poor black kid from the west side of Rockford who spent most of his adult life in prison).

But that's what the love of Christ can do for people. It brings them together and makes their differences go away.

Pastor Jonathan Byrd. The first thing I think of is his infectious laugh and my husband's impersonation of it. I think of the sermon where he preached about "Shadrach, Meshach and 'a BAD Negro.'" I think about all the amazing things I know about his life and how God literally picked him up out of his past and plunked him down in the future. I think about how God saved him time and time again… literally made bullets stop in the gun barrel… literally put a wedge between a man's knife and his heart… literally saved him, because God knew this man would serve him. God knew this man was marked to do amazing things, to turn lives around… to make a difference with his remarkable testimony.

A few years ago, I started meeting with Pastor Byrd on a regular basis. With tape recorder and notepad in hand, I wrote down the details of his life. I heard about the amazing way in which God delivered him from a life of drugs and prostitution into a life of Jesus and His Holy Spirit.

I sat in awe as I heard the stories of his childhood — of being passed from grandparent to mother to a father he never knew. I tried not to cry as he talked about a stepfather who, in an effort to teach the young Jonathan a lesson, set him loose in a field and randomly shot bullets into the darkness. I tried to imagine the man I knew beating men for messing with his "investments" (prostitutes) or even high on heroin and cocaine. I couldn't believe I was speaking to the same person. I guess he is walking proof that Christ's love really CAN turn a life around.

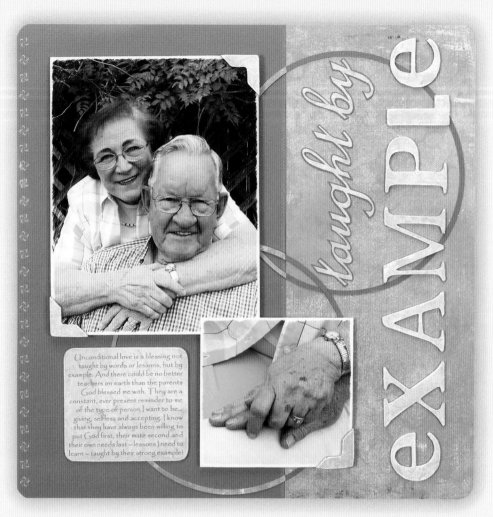

TAUGHT BY EXAMPLE

by Jodi Amidei

There's nothing more inspiring than a person who practices what they preach. Jodi's layout celebrates the example her parents have provided for her in terms of their solid walk of faith. Not only does her layout create a legacy preserving a good memory of her parents, but it also acts as a thank you to them for a job well done. We all know people who have been a wonderful example of how to live a right life. Have you thanked them? Create a page to express the traits you have learned from them and give it to them as a gift! You will undoubtedly touch their heart!

Thank you for living a faithful life everyday— even in the times when I am sure it was difficult. Thank you for teaching me the truth, but for showing it by following Christ in all the things you do... much love—

THANKS *by Hanni Baumgardner*

Few people in our lives have the kind of impact a parent has. When your parents model a good Christian life, there are hardly words to express the gratitude. Hanni's parents were a wonderful example to her, showing her how to live a righteous life. In this layout, she expresses her thankfulness, simply and to the point. How have your own parents impacted your walk of faith? Are there other people in your life who have guided you as a spiritual mother or father would? Why not make a page about them, thanking them for their example? You life wouldn't be the same without them.

Friendships play a huge part in our faith. Being surrounded by like-minded people helps keep us going in the right direction. We all have those friendships that go deeper than just the occasional hello. These friends inspire us to walk out our faith day by day.

pastor's wives

Very often, our friends can help keep us on track in terms of our faith. They hold us to our word. They listen to us vent. They tell us when we need to "get over it." For me, that group of friends happens to be the other pastors' wives at the church where my husband works. I value these friendships, and watching these women fulfill God's call on their lives inspires me to do the same. I don't know if I could handle the challenges and demands without these women and their understanding. How valuable this layout will be to me years from now, when I look back on this season of my life, knowing that I got through it in large part because of these women.

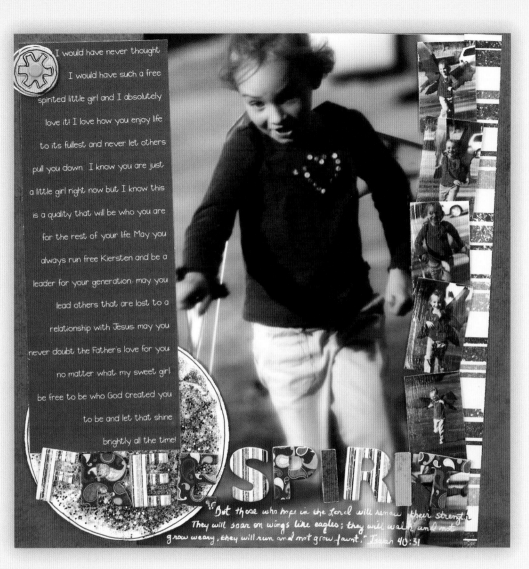

I would have never thought I would have such a free spirited little girl and I absolutely love it! I love how you enjoy life to its fullest and never let others pull you down. I know you are just a little girl right now but I know this is a quality that will be who you are for the rest of your life. May you always run free Kiersten and be a leader for your generation. may you lead others that are lost to a relationship with Jesus. may you never doubt the Father's love for you no matter what my sweet girl. be free to be who God created you to be and let that shine brightly all the time!

"But those who hope in the Lord will renew their strength. They will soar on wings like eagles; they will walk and not grow weary, they will run and not grow faint." Isaiah 40:31

Free Spirit *by Heather Preckel*

Wouldn't it be nice if we could carry the freedom of childhood into adulthood? It may be more difficult to stay free-spirited as we grow up, but watching her daughter inspired Heather to give it a try! This layout, showcasing a number of action shots, really captures the essence of childhood. The layout also serves almost as a prayer for Heather's daughter—that she'll never lose this trait her mommy loves so much.

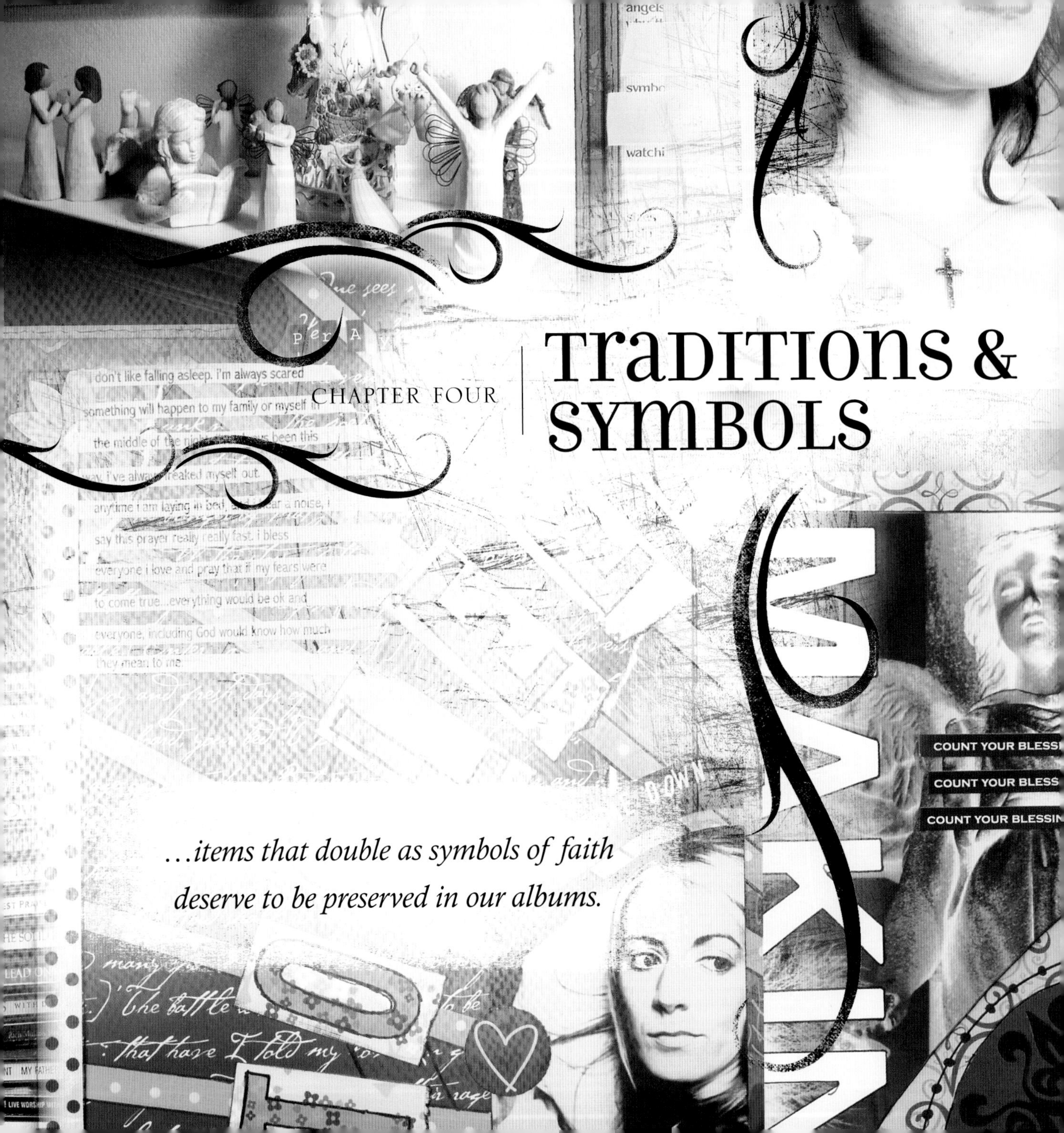

CHAPTER FOUR

TRADITIONS & SYMBOLS

…items that double as symbols of faith
deserve to be preserved in our albums.

i don't like falling asleep. i'm always scared
something will happen to my family or myself
the middle of the night as been this
i've always freaked myself out.
anytime i am laying in bed, a noise, i
say this prayer really really fast. i bless
everyone i love and pray that if my fears were
to come true...everything would be ok and
everyone, including God would know how much
they mean to me.

COUNT YOUR BLESS

COUNT YOUR BLESS

COUNT YOUR BLESSIN

MOST religions are BUILT on tradition. There is something comforting about singing the songs our ancestors sang, or reciting the same words they once said. The history of our religions is hugely important to their future. From baptisms to communion to fasting and prayer, church traditions link people across the world. They unite believers, giving them a common ground on which to build, a commonality that is rarely duplicated.

As much as we cling to our traditions, we also latch on to the symbols of our faith. Typically, religious people are proud of their faith, and they like to show it off. From bumper stickers, to jewelry, to plaques hanging on our walls, items that double as symbols of faith deserve a place in our albums.

Passing along the appreciation for our religious traditions and symbols is important to the preservation of our religion. Without these aspects, religion wouldn't last. It wouldn't continue. People would fail to see the importance. Knowing we are standing alongside hundreds and thousands of others who shared our beliefs, worshipping in the same way they worshipped, gives our faith a heavier weight and a whole new dimension.

BUT WHY?
THE BOTTOM LINE:

Religious traditions and symbols can seem pretty silly if you aren't a part of said religion. Debunk all the myths and allow future generations to instead get a glimpse of the inner-workings of your faith. Take the mystery away so it seems more tangible, more accessible. Don't make everyone wonder why you wore that cross necklace or had a tattoo of shooting stars on your shoulder. *Tell them in your pages.*

Consider walking the halls of your church on a day when there is no service going on. The quietness or busyness may surprise you. What kind of feeling do you get inside? Have you thought about all the other people who have walked through its doors?

come Home

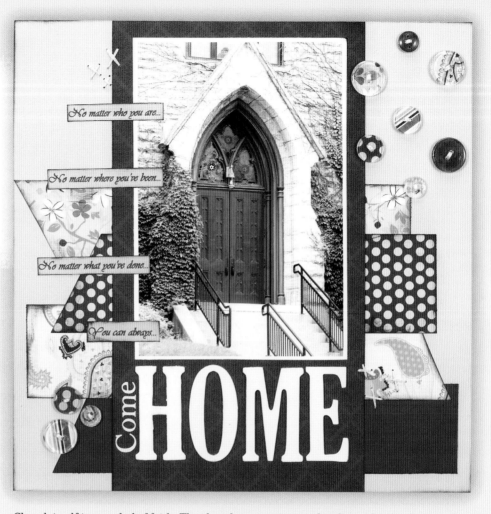

Church itself is a symbol of faith. The church you go to says a lot about what you believe. It says a lot about where you are in your life. Many people shy away from church because they feel they aren't "cleaned up enough" to attend. I wanted to create this page to convey the message that it doesn't matter what your past is—the only thing that matters is the future. I love that God accepts us with open arms at our very lowest point in life, and that church isn't a place only for the righteous. What do you love about church? As a symbol, what does it represent to you?

This is a Prayer

i don't like falling asleep. i'm always scared something will happen to my family or myself in the middle of the night. i've always been this way. i've always freaked myself out.

anytime i am laying in bed, and i hear a noise, i say this prayer really really fast. i bless everyone i love and pray that if my fears were to come true...everything would be ok and everyone, including God would know how much they mean to me.

SLEEP LOST

AS I LAY ME DOWN.

lay me down to sleep *by Amber Clark*

Some childhood prayers often stick with us well into adulthood, comforting us in a way that nothing else really can. For Amber, this common children's prayer is more than just words she learned in Sunday school. Anytime she feels afraid, she simply recites this prayer and remembers God is near. Many religions have recitations and prayers that can become a huge source of strength when we need them most. A layout like Amber's will serve as an excellent record of these prayers.

Every Child Receives This name and blessing to Give them an idea of what awaits them in their years to come. Promises, hopes, things they can use to be all they are foreordained to.

Rebekah Lynn Henderson blessed May 21st 2006 by her father La... Henderson

Born to Two parents Sent straight from Heaven. A name And A Blessing to Start your Time on Earth

BLESSING DAY

by Ruth Akers

Blessing Day. Baptism Day. Christening. No matter what your religion calls it, it's a tradition no parent will soon forget. For those who live a religious life, committing a child back to Christ is one of the most important rituals we have. As Ruth's layout demonstrates, it's also one we won't want to forget. It's often difficult to get a great photo in a church, but don't let that stop you from documenting this important tradition. Use a photo of the baby, as Ruth has done here, and simply include the details of the Blessing Day in your journaling.

Eggstravaganza

...a church tradition.

About 5 or 6 yrs ago our church started an Easter tradition in Eggstravaganza. At the time, we had no idea in just a few short years, we would be in charge of carrying on this tradition. Our kids love the Easter Egg hunt, the prizes & after years of refusals, the photo with the Easter bunny. I love the social traditions at our church. I love that it gives them a safe place to play I know they will always remember

EGGSTRAVAGANZA

Some church traditions beg to be taken seriously. No laughing allowed. Others, however, are full of fun! The social side of church is one I value, and it seems like the more you do something, the more people expect it. Before you know it, you've got a new tradition on your hands. We have several social traditions at our church, and I don't want to forget any of them! I love that they are going to be a huge part of the memories my family is creating in this season of our lives.

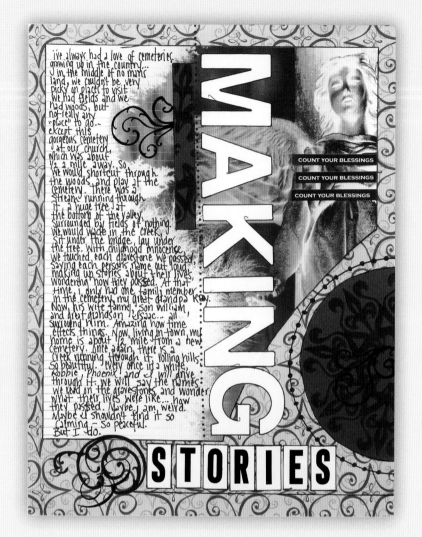

i've always had a love of cemeteries. growing up in the country... in the middle of no man's land, we couldn't be very picky on places to visit. we had fields and we had woods, but not really any "places" to go... except this gorgeous cemetery at our church, which was about 1/2 a mile away. so we would shortcut through the woods, and play at the cemetery. there was a stream running through it, a huge tree at the bottom of the valley, surrounded by fields of nothing. we would wade in the creek, sit under the bridge, lay under the tree. With childhood innocence, we touched each gravestone we passed, saying each persons name out loud, making up stories about their lives, wondering how they passed. At that time, I only had one family member in the cemetery, my great grandpa Ray. Now, his wife Fanny, son William, and great grandson Issac... all surround him. Amazing how time effects things. Now, living in town, my home is about 1/2 mile from a new cemetery. Once again, there is a creek running through it, rolling hills. so beautiful. every once in a while, Robbie, Phoenix and I will drive through it. we will say the names we read on the gravestones, and wonder what their lives were like... how they passed. Maybe I am weird. Maybe I shouldn't find it so calming - so peaceful. But I do.

MAKING

COUNT YOUR BLESSINGS
COUNT YOUR BLESSINGS
COUNT YOUR BLESSINGS

STORIES

making
stories

by Amber Clark

Some traditions aren't rooted in religion, but they bring us a peace that can only come from God. That is the case with Amber's tradition of visiting cemeteries and making up stories about the people resting there. A tradition that goes back to childhood, the practice is something Amber has passed on to her own son. Many of our traditions are ones that other people might not understand. They are personal, and therefore deserve a place in our personal scrapbooks. Do you have any childhood traditions that still bring you a sense of peace today? Pass it along to your children, and document it for posterity's sake.

CTR *by Ruth Akers*

What better way to remind yourself of your faith than to wear a symbol of its teachings on your hand? Every time Ruth looks at this ring, she is reminded of the principles it stands for. This CTR ring is a symbol of faith that Ruth treasures. It reminds her to "choose the right." People have these sort of "anchors" in all different types and forms. Whether it's a rock carried in your pocket, a cross on your neck, or a ring you wear, these symbols help keep us grounded in what we believe. What are some symbols you hold on to that remind you of what you believe?

Is anyone among you sick? Let him call for the elders of the church, and let them pray over him, anointing him with oil in the name of the Lord. And the prayer of faith will save the sick, and the Lord will raise him up. And if he has committed sins, he will be forgiven. — James 5:14-15

Our church believes in James 5:14 - 15. If you're sick, you have the elders of the church pray over you, anointing you with oil. This tradition may seem old fashioned, but it's powerful - even for today. I've seen this work on so many occasions, it's strengthened my faith and helped me believe - beyond a shadow of a doubt - that there is power in our prayers.

THE POWER OF PRAYER

THE POWER OF PRAYER

Churches in America are full of traditions. Even the most contemporary churches have certain things they do every time they gather together. For our church, praying for the sick is one of those traditions. It's important to me because so many times it's been the tool God has used to move in my life. What traditions does your church have and how do they affect you personally? What do you want future generations to know about the way things are done today?

anything BUT

traditional

ANYTHING BUT TRADITIONAL

People who are used to traditional churches might be thrown at first when they visit mine. The lack of tradition is one of the things I love about it, however. While many churches are full of ritual and ceremony, my church is more modern and contemporary. The absence of tradition is every bit as important to document as the traditions themselves. Choosing a church based on tradition (or the lack thereof) is a huge part of the story of your faith. Be sure to include that aspect of your story.

People might not understand why we raise our hands during praise and worship. It's such an important part of our faith, and yet, so many people just don't get it. Raising your hands in worship is an act of surrender. It's a visible sign that you are giving God the control to your life. I learned the hard way that it's much easier to start off with God in control. My way is not the best way. He always knows better than me. I don't raise my hands in worship to try and make a point or to pretend I'm more into it than I am. I raise my hands because it's my heart's cry - more than anything - to be fully surrendered to God's will in my life. Without that, I am nothing. I can do nothing. Lord, I surrender.

surrender

Why do we lift our hands? As a kid, I always wondered. No one really explained it—we just did it. I'm older now, and I have kids of my own. That makes me think about all the questions they might have. I don't want them to wonder about the reasons we do things at church. If it's important to our faith, I want them to understand it. I love watching kids worship. When they get it, it's a powerful sight. The act of surrendering is important. It occurred to me they won't get it unless we explain it. That's why I created this page. It's written explanation of the reason behind the symbol.

"Where do you go to church?"
"We home church"
"Oh that is interesting...how did you get into that?"

That is usually the response I get when asked that question and it never surprises me. Especially since we live in the bible belt with a church literally on every corner! We had always attended non-denominational churches our whole married life and had great experiences in them. There is just something about meeting together on a Sunday morning and having praise and worship together and then a good message. It filled the need we had in our lives for a long time.

But something started to change in us a few years ago; a yearning and longing to go deeper in our relationships and not just the average "hey how are you" you usually get on a Sunday morning. We had good friends but many we would just see on Sundays and there just seemed to be something missing; something deep and meaningful that our souls longed for.

Sunday mornings started to become a big chore for us and we didn't look forward to them as much. Our hearts were changing and we really didn't know what to do about it.

It was around this time that we started a small group with about 10 other people that had a longing just like ours; a longing to go deeper than your typical Sunday morning. We started meeting on a week night and the Lord really started doing something. We had no real time agenda and really just came together to wait on Him; and great things started happening. People seemed to leave their agendas at the door and really started opening up to the great things that were happening. I think the casual atmosphere was something that people felt more comfortable in and their guards were coming down to see what was on the inside of their hearts. Our heart's desire was to truly know the people we called our friends and that the Lord would touch us all in a deep way through those relationships and it was starting to happen. We all started looking forward to this time and Sunday church had less and less of a pull on us; this was becoming our church.

Then the church we were all attending starting noticing our meetings and become very interested in what was happening with us. They even took a huge step and decided to close down their big Sunday meeting and go to smaller home services in the area. It seemed to work for a little bit but our little group was broken up and we all missed what the Lord had been doing with us. We missed the intimacy that we all had together; the opening up and sharing our deep personal feelings. That is something that takes time and just doesn't happen because you start a small group. We all felt called to be together in this manner and when we were pulled apart to help other small groups it began to feel like BIG church again with groups of people that were just going along for the ride.

So after a short time we all decided to end our individual home groups and come back together with a small group that had been together before. That was 3 years ago and we are still meeting and it is wonderful! There is just something about getting together with a group of people that you know genuinely care for you and what happened during your week and you can sit and talk to them face to face and not just stare at the back of their head. Big church is a wonderful thing and we occasionally still attend one for the big praise and worship we miss out on but for us home church is our hearts and deep longing and it works for us.

I don't think we could ever go back to the way we used to be and for me that is quite all right. There is just something about meeting in a small intimate group of people that you can't get on a Sunday morning. At least it was something we couldn't find. We love the freedom we have to share our hearts; to be who we are; to explore what God is speaking into each of our lives; to be free to cry and laugh and play. It is the best thing for us and something we are so very thankful for.

Home Church

HOME CHURCH *by Heather Preckel*

Church is a typical symbol of faith, but for Heather, her church experience is anything but typical. In this layout, she recounts her family's decision to begin holding church services in their home. While their decision may seem unconventional, according to Heather, they know they are right where God wants them. This small group of people provides their family with a unique church experience she knew she wanted to document in her scrapbook. "It is wonderful to go to 'church' with a group of people that care about every area of your life and desire the best for you," Heather says. "I wouldn't want it any other way."

What a priceless gift,
undeserved life

Have I been given,
Through Christ crucified

You've called me out of death,
You've called me into life,

+ I was under your wrath
Now through the cross,
I'm reconciled.

At the cross you beckon me
You draw me gently to my
knees, and I am lost

for words, so lost in love, I'm
sweetly broken,
wholly surrendered.

— Jeremy Riddle

AT THE CROSS

by Hanni Baumgardner

The cornerstone of the Christian faith is the symbol of the cross. Held in the highest regard, the cross is not only a pretty piece of jewelry, but a reminder of the ultimate sacrifice Christ made when He died. Hanni's layout uses song lyrics to convey her thoughts on this classic Christian symbol, making it known to anyone who reads the page that she believes in what it stands for. Often, the meaning behind common symbols is watered down as it hits the mainstream. If you want to maintain its importance, however, a layout like this one would be the perfect way to do so.

SONG OF MY SOUL *by Jodi Amidei*

One of the ultimate symbols of faith is music. A large collection of Christian CDs serves as
the focal point photo for Jodi's lovely page, but there's more to this layout than meets the eye.
For Jodi, music wasn't just something to provide background noise—it played a huge role in
ushering her into the next level of her faith. In this page, she tells of the important part
worship songs have had in her life. In times of mourning or joy, the music has always been
there. Music can enable us to really crave God's presence, as was the case with Jodi, and
thanks to this ever-expanding collection, it continues to do so.

trust

Safe Flight In Jesus' Name

Ever since I had kids, I don't travel well. I never used to be afraid to fly - in fact, I went through a brief stint where I thought for sure I would end up an astronaut or a pilot. But then I met Adam and my life suddenly wasn't about me anymore. After we had the kids, it got even harder to be away from them... especially if it meant I had to fly. My sister is quite accustomed to flying, and years ago she shared with me a tip that always got her through the anxiety attached to the airplane. As she boards a flight, she simply rests her hand on the outside of the plane and quietly says, "Safe flight in Jesus' Name." I instantly adopted this as my own personal flying tradition, covering the plane with the power that rests in the name of Jesus. Of course I'm careful not to be too loud - wouldn't want to offend anyone or freak anyone out... and really, I do it for myself. I know that I can rest once I've claimed my safety. I know that my inviting God to fly with me means the anxiety and fear have to go away. I suppose some would call this a superstition... but to me, a prayer is never a superstition. And this prayer, albeit short and to the point, is still a prayer... and now, it's a tradition I will likely have until the day I die. I am so relieved I can call on Jesus' name at any given moment and instantly his peace envelopes me like the arms of a Father. Thank you Lord, for flying the friendly skies with me. I couldn't do it without you!

safe FLIGHT

It may seem more like a superstition, but to me, prayer is always more than that. Even those quick prayers that are muttered under my breath on the way out the door. I created a layout about the prayer I pray every time I fly—a simple but important prayer that instantly puts me at peace. I have been doing this for so long, this is now a tradition for me. It may seem sort of silly to someone who doesn't share my beliefs, but I know that God is watching out for me, on the ground and in the air…especially when I ask Him to.

i don't really remember which one came first, but sometime after my daughter Sarah died, I started a collection of angels. I didn't know why they made me feel better, I just knew that they did. Now I know — it's because they are a symbol to me. They remind me each time I see them that I'm not alone — someone is watching over me!

So, I've filled my home with angels of all kinds, sizes and shapes to help me remember that I'm loved, cared about and constantly being watched over!

I BELIEVE someone's watching over me

someone's watching over me *by Jodi Amidei*

A simple reminder may be all you need to hold on to the promises of God. For Jodi, that reminder lies in her collection of angels—something that has given her peace since the death of her daughter. This collection is not only beautiful, but it's something she treasures for its deeper meaning. You may have a similar collection, or even just one trinket that reminds you of God's unfailing love. Photograph it and create a page about it. It is bound to become as cherished as the trinket itself.

What is the meaning behind your name? Your children's names? You might be surprised by the kind of clues they can give you about your character and personality. No one is here by accident, so your name means something! Unlock the mystery of your name and you may discover your purpose—a purpose that is worth reinforcing for yourself or your child on a scrapbook page that you can refer to again and again for strength.

named BY GOD

It took us a long time to find a name we felt would suit our first son, but when you were born, we knew you were an "Ethan." I believe our names signify so much of who we are and who we are called to be. I believe you are set apart to love the truth – to stand for the things you know are right, to be firm and steadfast. We didn't know it at the time, but we later discovered there was an Ethan in the Bible and he was a worship leader and musician. What a fitting name for the son of a musician. I believe your name is just a tiny clue of God's awesome plan for you. And we will continue to pray that plan will come to pass

named By GOD.

ethan
Origin: Hebrew
Inherent Meaning: "Firmness"
Spiritual Connotation: "Steadfast in Truth"

What's in a name? Well, a lot if you ask me. The Bible says He knew us in our mother's womb—He knew our name and the plan He has for our lives. For our son, we were hopeful he would be steadfast in the truth. It was one of the qualities we knew we wanted to see in him, so rather than just being a name we liked, "Ethan" became a symbol, almost a prayer. Now, every time we call him by name, we're solidifying those words and those qualities in him.

At first glance, my sister's tattoo might look like just another tattoo - the kind you'd see on lower backs of girls everywhere. But look closer. In the body of the butterfly, it says: '2C517'. A combination to a gym locker? Not quite. Something a little deeper. 2 Corinthians 5:17: 'If anyone is in Christ, he is a new creation. The old has gone, the new has come.' Carrie got this tattoo when she rededicated her life to the Lord. A permanent reminder that once you become a butterfly, you will never be a caterpillar again.

TATTOO OF FAITH

Tattoos are only for biker dudes, right? Not anymore, my friend. Tattoos are for everyone—and they are often a way to symbolize your faith. My sister's tattoo is more than just a pretty picture; it's a reminder that, like a butterfly, she is a new creation in Christ. The old is gone and the new has come. After all, once a caterpillar turns into a butterfly, it can't go back to being a caterpillar. Since she's not a scrapbooker, I do most of her memory keeping for her. Years from now, her grandchildren are going to get a huge kick out of the fact that their Gram has a big old tattoo on her back. Once they learn the meaning behind it, it will become a much more vivid symbol.

dream

BOY... GOD KNEW YOU WOULD MELT MY HEART.

CHAPTER FIVE | BLESSINGS

By focusing on your blessings, you will undoubtedly gain a new outlook on life.

thank-ful

that you are still here.

WHAT ARE YOU THANKFUL FOR? If you're like me, you can probably think of many things. From the people God has surrounded us with, to the homes we live in, to the very breath we have just taken, we have so many blessings. But in the busyness of life, how often do we stop to consider all the ways God has blessed us? A fleeting thought of gratitude isn't sufficient to really impact our lives.

By focusing on your blessings, you will undoubtedly gain a new outlook on life. Taking care to pay attention to the many ways God has provided for you, or simply given you something you wanted but never thought you could have, puts everything into perspective. There's an old hymn that goes: *Count your blessings, name them one by one, Count your blessings, see what God has done.*

Can you do it? Can you count all the amazing blessings in your life? I challenge you to try! Keep an album full of them. And in your darkest hour, think of another one and scrap it! Having all your blessings laid out in front of you leaves not only an important legacy, but also a reason to smile.

BUT WHY?
THE BOTTOM LINE:

Years ago, the idea of the "gratitude journal" was touted by Oprah Winfrey and women across the country. Oprah is a very wise woman. This idea can keep you grounded. It can ward off depression. It can help you focus on the positives instead of dwelling on the negatives. Blessings abound… they are everywhere! Grab a pen, start writing, and see how many you can list. Now, start putting them in a beautiful album. I guarantee *you will cherish it forever!*

Velcro is a versatile tool for creating hidden journaling. For this layout, my journaling was too long to include in the design, so I created a flap that opens underneath the row of three photos. They are held down by a small strip of Velcro. It's easy to open, and yet perfect for keeping things in place.

* Our Neighborhood * July 5th, 2003 *

God was with us... even in the eye of the storm.

MIRACULOUS

When I look at these pictures, it is an instant reminder of how blessed my family is. At the heart of the storm, with chaos and destruction all around us, we emerged completely unscathed. How does that happen? Every yard in our neighborhood had horrible damage—trees down, completely uprooted, some of them resting in the center of the house. But our home and land were fine. We had several trees on our property, but all were intact. It was scary to wake up and see our neighborhood in this condition, but mostly I was overwhelmed with gratefulness that God had been with us—watching over us in the storm.

Staying at home with the boys is a luxury I wouldn't exchange for anything, but... any mom would know that it's not really a glamourous life – jumping from one meal to nappy change and then to another... the routine and mundaneness can get pretty crazy. In the midst of all the business I've found little ways to sneak in moments of quiet. Like when we stop to observe butterflies, or pygmy hippos, or chimpanzees at the zoo. When we exchange names with our neighbour's kids. These moments allow me to pause and consider the vastness and variety evident of our natural world. They allow me to appreciate the presence of other people and keep them in my mind. They allow me to pause, meditate, and then praise and acknowledge the almighty presence of a God who is at work in our world. I think I might have completely missed out on this if I were leading a different kind of life.

TIME TO PAUSE *by Brenda-Mae Teo*

Having children is one of the greatest blessings of any life. But children don't come with an instruction booklet. They force us to grow up and learn a number of key lessons every day. For Brenda-Mae, learning to slow down and appreciate the little details of life was something she only did after being blessed with her two children. Those little details that enrich your life are so easy to miss if you don't slow down and look for them. When you catch them, though, they are some of life's greatest rewards.

Some blessings are really abstract, but others hit like a ton of bricks. Walking away from an accident completely uninjured is a definite blessing, worth thanking God for. Consider making a mini album or art journal full of blessings, both abstract and overt. Write down one thing you are thankful for each day—and force yourself to focus on the truly important things in your life.

BLESSING

I hate these pictures. I hate thinking about what could've been, had Adam not been covered in the blood of Jesus. I hate to remember that it was something for ME that even took him on that country road, where a young kid decided to pass in a no passing zone, on a hill, sending Adam off the road, but not without first broadsiding him. We took pictures in case we needed them for insurance reasons, but I actually use them for another purpose - to always remember God's goodness. To always be thankful for His provision, for his mercy. To never take one single day for granted, but instead... to praise Him for each breath He allows me to take. I know tomorrow is promised to no man, but I am SO thankful that it was promised to Adam on that day. Thank you, Jesus, for watching out for him. It would be tempting to look at this accident as something horrible, but instead, I think I'll continue to view it as a blessing. Even though it was expensive and the other driver wasn't insured, Adam is safe - and alive. That is the ultimate blessing.

Blessing of all blessings: emerging from a really bad accident completely unscathed. When Adam called to tell me he had just been in an accident, my heart raced. It was a reminder not to take any of it for granted—a wake-up call that we aren't here forever, that our lives are precious gifts, that my husband is a precious gift. Shaken up as I was, I was so thankful God had sent angels to guard Adam's car that day. I was so thankful I'd prayed for days prior that no harm would come to my husband. I was so thankful I got another day with the man I love. Blessed—there's no other way to describe it.

STORY OF GOD'S HOME *by Deb Perry*

One of the greatest blessings is watching God's hand in our lives. For Deb, He proved His care for her family by leading them down the woodsy path to this beautiful home. Deb watched in amazement as she learned to trust Him through an experience that would've had many people questioning His existence. In the end, it paid off, and her family now has a peaceful retreat of their own. This layout serves as a constant reminder to Deb and her family to thank God for His provision in their lives. What a wonderful testimony that He is watching over us—even when He is quiet!

How many times have you prayed for something only to have the complete opposite happen? How many times have you been wrong about what you thought you needed in your life? After getting over the initial disappointment, were you able to see a better plan for your life? Document these instances as reminders of how God blesses us even when it's not what we think we want.

He knew

He knew I nEedEd YOU

I thought I had it all figured out. Graduate college. Move to New York. Become an actress. Maybe get married around 29. Maybe have a kid around 32. Depending, of course, on my career. It's so funny looking back on it now. I don't feel like I gave up on my dream - not by any means... but I do feel like if I were living that life, knowing myself a little better now, I would be miserable. It was like everything I said I would never do. God said, "Oh, I think you might be surprised..." and dropped me in the middle of what I thought would be agony.

Turns out those things I didn't want - a husband, kids while I was young, to be a stay at home mom... those are the things that absolutely make me the happiest. Those are the things I couldn't live without. Those are the things that top my 'thank you' list. And He knew it all along. It's easy for me now to surrender my will to His, having seen that His will is so much better. I know that He knows what will ultimately make me happy... After all, he knew how much I needed these three. They are my greatest blessing.

Isn't it funny how we always assume we know what is best for us? Looking back on the things I used to pray for, things I used to *beg* God for, I am so glad that in the same breath I would ask for *His* will to be done in my life. That way, I wasn't left to my own devices! My biggest mistake was thinking I didn't want a husband and kids. I am so thankful God knew what a tremendous blessing these three people would be in my life—my greatest joy comes from them. He definitely knew what it would take to make me the happiest! And I, obviously, had *no* idea!

Land of the Free.
Home of the Brave.

One of the greatest blessings in my life is that I live in America. I live in a country where I can worship God any way I choose. I live in a land where freedom is of the utmost importance - something to be defended and fought for. I am so thankful I am an American.

LAND OF THE FREE

Having lived in America my entire life, it wasn't until recently I truly began to understand what it meant to be free. Free to worship however I choose is one blessing I never want to take for granted. Tied into my heritage, I feel like this layout is so important to my story. I value religious freedom. I realize now that not everyone is so fortunate. Not everyone is allowed to worship the God of their choice in the way they want to. If I really sit and think about that, I am overwhelmed with gratitude to live in a country that allows me that freedom. I am so thankful to be an American.

Proverbs 27:17 says, "As iron sharpens iron, so one man sharpens another."

sharpen.

We are surrounded by people who sharpen us. For different reasons and in different ways, each of these people has made us stronger in Christ. All part of the staff at our church, these people have challenged us — both personally and in our ministry. I am so thankful for like-minded friends who will build us up — pray for us — push us to excel and reach the next level… and then push us even more. Our staff is young… but they are wise. I am so thankful for the iron God has surrounded us with.

sharpen

One of the greatest blessings in my life has got to be the people. And while many people inspire us, there is a whole different group of people who challenge us—sharpen us—help us to become better in our ministry and in our Christian walk. These people just happen to be on staff at our church. While they have impacted us in different ways, they've all brought us to the next level, opened our eyes to see God's faithfulness in a way we would've missed otherwise. And who knew you could actually love your co-workers? "As iron sharpens iron…" so have these men and women sharpened us.

In October of 2004, we almost lost my Mom. Diverticulitis led to a severe abdominal infection which led to a hospital stay we'd all love to forget. I didn't realize at the time how serious it was, which is probably a good thing. You see, this woman is not just my mother... she is my best friend. I am so blessed to have a mom who was born to care for other people. This photo was taken that Thanksgiving... Looking at it I am reminded to thank God for the blessing of life. Not just mine... but the lives of those I love. So blessed it wasn't her time to go. So blessed God healed her... because it'll be a long time before I'm ready to say good-bye. thank you God. thank you.

so so **thank-ful**

that you are still here.

november '04

thank you. thank you. thank you. thank you. thank you. thank you.

SO THANKFUL

When I look at this photo, I can still see the sickness in my mom's eyes. She doesn't normally look tired, but after ten days in the hospital, that Thanksgiving was a hard one. The magnitude of thankfulness was heightened more than ever when the doctor told her they almost lost her. We almost lost her. As I kicked into emergency mode, I forgot to be really thankful she was going to be OK. It wasn't until later that it hit me. I am so blessed by this woman. She has been a true example of love and selflessness in my life. So not only am I thankful to have her as a mom, but I'm thankful to still have her.

This photo could easily become part of my Thanksgiving layout for that year, but when I see it, I see something deeper. I see the blessing of life. Sometimes we focus so much on the event, we forget we can pull photos from that event and talk about how they make us feel. Find the story within the story and scrap that too. After all, it's in your stories that you're really going to leave a part of yourself behind.

I fit here

Faith Center is my home. These people have given me a place where I know I fit in. They trust us. They support us. And we finally understand that this ministry is more than just a job... it's a calling.

I FIT

Growing up, we all have those seasons where we feel awkward and out of place. What a wonderful blessing to finally feel like you fit in, and you are just exactly where God wants you. Finally, that is how I feel. I know this staff at our church is a group that God has assembled for a common purpose, and being a part of that is one of the greatest blessings of my life. Church groups, community clubs—even scrapbookers coming together once a month to crop—are all examples of where you might feel you fit in. Think about the peace and the joy you feel when you are in that element. A blessing worth noting!

mama to a monkey

When I was pregnant with my son, I was certain I was carrying a very large girl. I already had a girl, so it seemed natural to imagine myself with another one. It wasn't until about a week before Ethan was born that I began to entertain the idea he could actually be a boy. I started to sort of panic, afraid there was no way I could be a mother to a *boy*. But now that he's three, and I understand how unique the relationship between a mother and her son is, I realize I am so glad I was wrong. God knew being a mother to this little monkey would make my life more complete. He knew this would be one of my greatest blessings.

one BABY, FIVE MIRACLES

Miracles might be a bit more subtle than they were in the Bible, but they are definitely still prevalent today. When my niece was born with a lump on her back, instant panic set in. Soon, God calmed everyone, and we sat back and watched Him work a mighty miracle in this little body. Emery should have problems, many problems, but she doesn't. It's been a year, and according to the doctors, she shouldn't be able to walk. And this little one doesn't do much walking—she's more often running! *That* is a tremendous blessing, and a visible miracle. I know there will be times in my life when my faith may waiver, when I may have a hard time believing, but the miracles I have witnessed first-hand will build my faith.

There's so much to Emery's story, I'm not quite sure how to start. It's hard to know how much detail to include in a story that is so miraculous. My niece was born in April of 2005. She was one of two babies delivered to my sister on that day. They were born in Georgia, which was hard for me because I couldn't be there with them. It was even harder when the doctors discovered a lump on Emery's back. It was the size of a lemon, and, of course, their first thought was a tumor.

Thankfully, first thoughts aren't always right. While doctors knew it wasn't a tumor, they didn't know exactly what it was... which is why it's surprising they wanted to do surgery to remove it on a six week old baby. Still, Matt and Carrie scheduled the surgery and prayed that somehow God would show them what to do. The day of the surgery came, and the doctors struggled so hard with getting the proper tubes in Emery that they decided to postpone the surgery, but they needed to reschedule right away.

I am so glad Matt and Carrie can hear the voice of God. They simply did not feel right about this surgery, and knew they were supposed to wait. Even though they were chastised for their decision, they stood firm. They were in the process of moving back to Illinois and decided to take her to see a doctor up here.

That was miracle #1.

Once they got settled, they began seeing a doctor at Children's Memorial Hospital in Chicago. The doctor explained exactly what the lump was. Emery's spinal cord hadn't closed and fat cells got inside, creating a lump. Furthermore, she wouldn't be able to have surgery until she was six months old - much older than the six weeks the doctors in Georgia required. Tests were ordered and the doctor was astounded. Even though the lump should've been causing Emery a number of problems, specifically with her bladder, there were none.

That was miracle #2.

Finally, Emery was six months and the waiting was over. Carrie was so ready for the lump to be gone. It never hurt Emery or bothered her at all, but Matt & Carrie didn't want her to have to deal with it anymore. They wanted to put the surgery behind them. Emery went in early on a Tuesday morning and had her lump removed. They weren't sure if they could get it all or if they would run into nerve problems, but everything went perfectly.

That was miracle #3.

When we went to visit them in the hospital, we asked for her bed and the nurses told us how cute my niece was. Everyone in the hospital hung around this tiny little baby, because even after having a lump dug out of her back, this little girl was still perfectly happy. Perfectly content. I couldn't believe the smiles I got from her. It was as though she felt no pain.

That was miracle #4.

The doctor told Matt and Carrie that within a few weeks, Emery's back would be virtually flat. So they waited. They got frustrated. Why wasn't it shrinking? And then... one day, as if it happened overnight... that lump began to shrink. There is very little trace of any kind of problem, and Emery continues to light up every room she's in.

That was miracle #5.

I've never had to go through anything like this with my own children, but the strength and faith my sister and brother-in-law displayed during such a trying time was a huge inspiration to me and to everyone around us. This baby will forever hold such a special place in my heart. She is cooing proof that miracles do happen... even nowadays... and that is something I am so thankful for.

FOCUS on FAITH

Sometimes when we're going through something, we don't think to document the "before." We fear there may never be an "after." But I knew I wanted to photograph the lump on Emery's back because it wasn't going to be there forever. Don't forget to photograph the hard things, even the ugly things, we're faced with. You never know when they are going to be proof that God is a healing God.

If I had to grow up... which I guess I did, I'm so glad I got to do it with these two. I am so thankful I wasn't an only child. Through the years, I've learned so much about myself and other people thanks to my siblings. My brother got my through high school - my sister brought me closer to the Lord - they both continue to challenge me and inspire me in different ways, and even though I cannot believe we are this old... I am so happy I am old with them.

GROWN UP.

grown up

Many of my biggest blessings are found in the relationships I value most. Two people who I absolutely treasure are my brother and sister. Having grown up the middle child, you would think I would resent them in some way—after all, isn't the middle child always the one who's passed over? But these two made my childhood memorable. More importantly, they've made my adulthood rich with a sense of family and love. They are part of my legacy, a huge part, and one I want future generations to get to know.

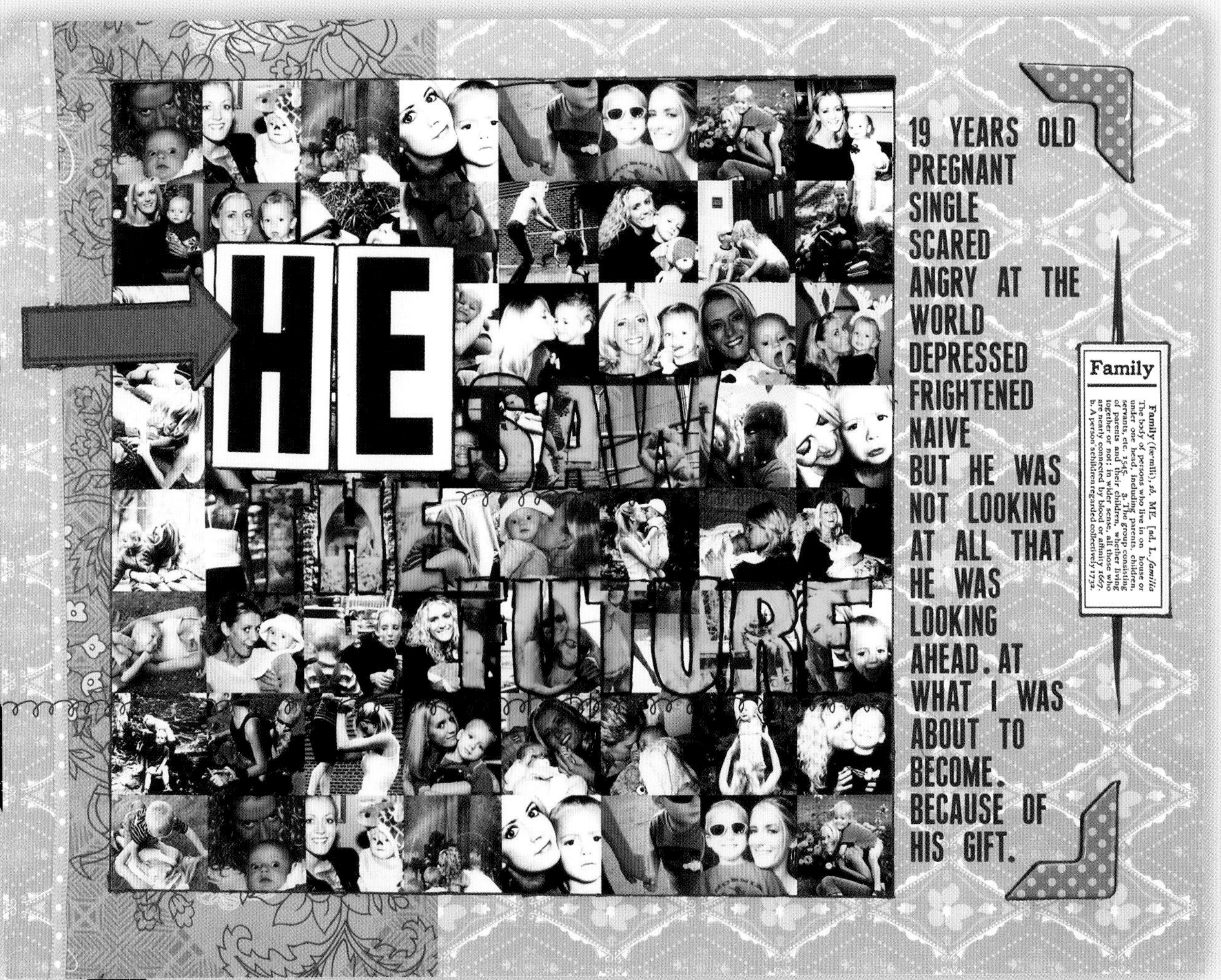

19 YEARS OLD PREGNANT SINGLE SCARED ANGRY AT THE WORLD DEPRESSED FRIGHTENED NAIVE BUT HE WAS NOT LOOKING AT ALL THAT. HE WAS LOOKING AHEAD. AT WHAT I WAS ABOUT TO BECOME. BECAUSE OF HIS GIFT.

HE SAW THE FUTURE

Family

Family (fĕr-mĭl), sb. ME. [ad. L. familia]

HE SAW THE FUTURE *by Amber Clark*

Isn't it amazing how God can take the thing that seems so crazy to the rest of the world and make it the best and brightest part of our lives? That was the case with Amber when she found out she was pregnant with her son. Of course, she didn't know at the time it would turn out the way it did, but God knew. He saw into the future—a young girl who would grow into a woman, all for the little man she would grow to love. Amber's layout, featuring snippets of photos of the two of them over the years is an honest look at her life, and a huge part of her story. Her son will never question that his mom sees him as the greatest gift of her life.

two babies at the same time would freak most people out, but not carrie. she's been praying for twins since she was a little girl. these two babies are more than a blessing; they are an answer to prayer.

DOUBLE BLESSING

They say there is power in the words we speak. Many believe we can actually speak things into existence. I have to say, having witnessed my sister's remarkable true confession, I'm not sure I disagree. Having said for years she wanted twins, my sister was still a bit shocked to find out there were two babies growing in her tummy. Two children who will grow together and bring double the joy to our family. Sometimes life's biggest blessings are those we never expected, and sometimes they are the things we always wished for but never dreamed we could obtain. Whatever the case, these blessing are worth documenting.

THANKS for my time at this place. im trying everyday to make the most of it. my family, my friends, my thoughts, my tears. They are all making this journey an amazing discovery. Each day my blessings teach me something new... + for that I am grateful. ♥ ME

HAPPINESS

dEaR GOD.

dEaR GOD *by Amber Clark*

Simple blessings. The little things. The things we often take for granted. *Don't* let them pass by unnoticed. Document them as Amber has done in this sweet layout that doubles as a prayer of thanks. Using a simple photo that shows her enjoying her life, Amber conveys the message that life is good. I'd be willing to bet your life is pretty good too. Break it down to the basics, because when the world gets dark, you'll still have those to rely on. And that could be what gets you through the storm.

kept

... and you knew me before I was
... and you sought me in the darkness
... and you found me when I could not find myself

... and you held me like a secret
... and you whispered by your spirit
... that you kept me for this moment and beyond.

now & forever

KEPT

I don't have the kind of testimony that would make a good Hollywood drama, but knowing that God kept me for this man and this day and this life is testimony enough. This was the moment I first saw Adam at our wedding. I remember wondering if he was regretting his choice. I also remember being so thankful I'd been taught to save myself for marriage. God knew there was the perfect person out there for me, and I was able to save myself for him. Kept. For this moment and beyond. I can't think of many blessings I treasure more than this one. (Words are from the song "Kept," by Debra Arnott.)

Before & After Blessing

What can I really say about this blessing? When Robin was selected to go on TLC's "What Not To Wear," we all knew God's favor was on her. A tiny woman, Robin has always struggled to find clothes to really fit her. So, instead of paying big bucks for alterations, Robin settled for hand me downs. She looked like an old lady, and she's still in her 30s! Her trip to New York was just what the doctor ordered. She came back a living testimony to God's goodness.

She was full of stories of how He had provided for her, giving her this once in a lifetime opportunity to be treated like a queen. It was such a wonderful thing to witness someone so deserving being blessed in such a hugely public way. Robin proved that God's unmerited favor is something you can't earn. You walk in it. And it's on her knowing that our God is that good - that gracious - to be concerned with something that may seem frivolous, but really makes such a difference was truly eye-opening. We had so much fun participating in this whole process. And we are blessed by Robin's blessing.

WHAT **NOT** TO WEAR

BEFORE AND AFTER BLESSING

Every once in awhile, you get to take part in something that is so unforgettable, there's no way *not* to document it. I knew I would want to create a layout to document the favor of the Lord on our friend, Robin, when she was chosen as "Chicago's worst dressed teacher." She was flown to New York and made over in a major way on national television. It was proof that God likes to bless us big time. The story is one I want other people to know about too because it's proof that when you're least expecting it, God will reward you. He'll reward you with things you may have originally thought were frivolous, just because He wants to love on you a little bit. I can't think of a better example of goodness.

So much of what I've learned over the years
is because of principles I've been taught
at church or in reading my Bible.

ing that doesn't matter, but I'm telling you... it does. Once
nce you decide the kind of person you want to be and the
promise that. Look at Daniel. He never compromised who
ot even for the king - and God rewarded him for it. God
s the same with you, Ethan. You can be a Daniel. You can

THE OLDER I GET, THE MORE I REALIZE how little I knew before. Every day, I learn something new. Another lesson to catalog in my brain and never forget—hopefully anyway—so I don't have to learn it all over again. Many of these lessons, I've discovered, are tied to my faith. So much of what I've learned over the years is because of principles I've been taught at church or in reading my Bible. So much of what God wants me to know, He's already taught someone in my path, and then they generously share their knowledge with me.

We all make mistakes. Some of them are worth noting because of what we learned from them. Others, of course, we'd just as soon forget. Through our faith, we learn a lot about right and wrong. We learn about forgiveness and unconditional love. Then there are those tiny nuggets of truth we learn that may not change our every day, but definitely change the person we are. Those nuggets are worth noting. Someone, somewhere, someday will learn that lesson because of you... but how can they if you never write it down?

BUT WHY?
THE BOTTOM LINE:

History is doomed to repeat itself. Isn't that what they say? Isn't that why they teach us history, so we can learn what other people did and either do the same, or avoid their mistakes? It's the same for you. You don't have to be Napoleon or FDR or John F. Kennedy to have something to contribute in the way of advice. This is your legacy you're leaving. If you died tomorrow, what *words of wisdom* would you want attributed to you? Scrapbook them!

Bible stories are great teaching tools for kids. Take your favorites and apply them to their lives. It will make the Word of God more applicable—more real to them—giving them a life-long appreciation for the Bible.

It might seem like the kind of thing that doesn't matter, but I'm telling you... it does. Once you know what you believe - once you decide the kind of person you want to be and the life you want to live - don't compromise that. Look at Daniel. He never compromised who he was and what he believed - not even for the lions - and God rewarded him for it. God protected him because of it. It's the same with you, Ethan. You can be a Daniel. You can praise God with your whole heart - even when it's not the popular thing or the cool thing - it will always be the right thing. Don't compromise. Your reward is great in heaven.

NEVER COMPROMISE.
GOD WILL REWARD YOU FOR IT.

never compromise

The book of Daniel is full of examples on excellent leadership. Perhaps the most important lesson I have taken away from the book is that Daniel never compromised. He knew what he believed, and he stuck to it. I have so much respect for a person who can stand their ground in the face of adversity—and I'd say a den of hungry lions was adversity of the worst kind! I want to pass this lesson on to my son. I want him to know it's OK to stand up for what he believes. At his young age, I see a boldness in him that I hope he can hold onto, and leading him to the book of Daniel will help.

TRUST *by Brenda-Mae Teo*

Every parent has experienced the tantrum to end all tantrums. As Brenda-Mae tried to calm her son down, she wondered why he wouldn't simply sit and listen to her? It would've saved them both so much emotional strain. However, in dealing with her son, she learned an important lesson. As we try to do things our own way, our Heavenly Father sits back, and wonders when we'll ever learn to trust Him. Through this experience, Brenda-Mae learned about the role of God as a parent. Sometimes in our stubbornness, we forget to listen. With this layout as a reminder, next time she will simply be able to trust.

If you aren't the only one with something faith-related to leave behind, consider having your spouse or even a grandparent write a letter to you or your children on the topic of faith—lessons they have learned because of their faith. Having additional perspectives represented in your albums is a great way to broaden the scope of who your pages reach.

yes, jesus loves you

Lessons of life for our sweet children.

yes
jesus
♥'s
you

And so do we.

There are so many sources in this world coming at our children every day. Many will try to convince these kids they aren't loved and that God doesn't care about them. I firmly disagree. I wanted my children to hear our voices, encouraging them and telling them the truth: Jesus does love them and He did die for them. My husband and I both wrote letters with some of our favorite life lessons so no matter what, our kids will always know how important they are to God…and to us.

Mixed nuts.
Ever notice how
When you get nothing
But the cashews
or the
Walnuts it only
takes a
Handful before you
Want to stop eating?
Take those same
cashews
And mix them
With the rest
of the
Nuts and dont you enjoy
The flavor even more?
So goes the life
of a mother.
You take the
good, with the
Bad. For without,
the bad,
You do not
Fully appreciate
The good. And well,
really
Arent we all a
little bit
Mixed nuts

2 teach

FOCUS on FAITH

What kind of insight do you have about the areas of your life that would be easy to resent? How has God helped you flip your thought process? Consider a mini album based on how God has turned frustrations into blessings—if you think about it, it happens a lot more than you realize!

MIXED NUTS *by Ruth Akers*

The life of a mother is full of its ups and its downs. Ruth's insightful page uses a bit of humor to convey a very important message: Without the bad, the good isn't quite as sweet. As a mom, it's easy to get frustrated with the monotony of daily life, the screaming child, the accidents involving bodily fluids. But if it weren't for those maddening moments, the moments of cuddles and coos would be far less meaningful.

A LETTER TO MYSELF

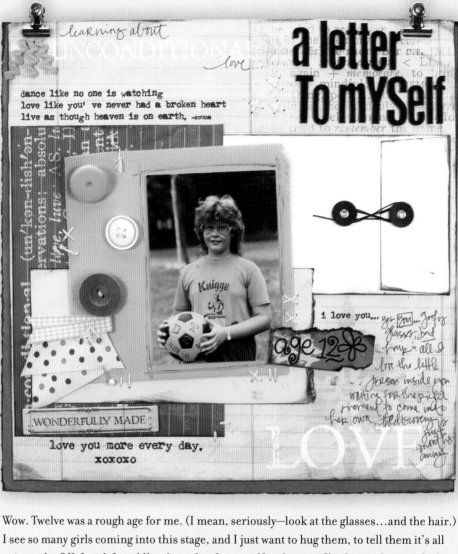

learning about UNCONDITIONAL love...

a letter To mYSelf

dance like no one is watching
love like you've never had a broken heart
live as though heaven is on earth. -souza

Knigge

age 12

WONDERFULLY MADE

love you more every day,
xoxoxo

i love you... yes You... goofy glasses and braces all I love the little person inside you waiting for the right moment to come into her own, the discovery is just months away

LOVE

Wow. Twelve was a rough age for me. (I mean, seriously—look at the glasses…and the hair.) I see so many girls coming into this stage, and I just want to hug them, to tell them it's all going to be OK. I wish I could've done that for myself at that age. I've learned so much about loving myself since this era of self-loathing. And every once in awhile, I still feel like I'm stuck in this age, self-conscious and awkward. So, I wrote a letter to my 12-year-old self. And in that letter, I told myself everything I wished I'd known. Everything I want my own daughter to know when she turns 12. Everything I need to remember in order to really see myself through God's eyes, and to love myself unconditionally. I think I'll be reading this letter a lot.

dear 12-year old courtney.

There's so much i would love to tell you, but let me start with this... the pain you're feeling right now won't last forever. You won't always struggle to fit in.

Look, I can't tell you your best friend is going to suddenly start being nice to you again... she won't. But, years from now, she will apologize — and you'll forgive her.

I can't tell you you'll snag a boyfriend anytime soon, It will be years from now before you have that first kiss. (Three, to be exact.) I can tell you once you do give your heart away, it will be forever.

I can't tell you everything will come easily. It won't. But the challenges you face will bring successes... and self esteem & one day you'll start to believe in your heart you can do anything.

I wish I could show you how much God loves you. I wish I could get it in your head that he created you in His image - for a purpose - for a reason. I wish you knew you are fearfully + wonderfully made. Because you are. Someday... you'll understand, but for now, just know you are okay.
                    love, 30-year old courtney

WORRY is faith in the Enemy.

"Therefore I tell you, do not worry about your life, what you will eat or drink; or about your body, what you will wear. Is not life more important than food, and the body more important than clothes? Look at the birds of the air; they do not sow or reap or store away in barns, and yet your heavenly Father feeds them. Are you not much more valuable than they? Who of you by worrying can add a single hour to his life? "And why do you worry about clothes? See how the lilies of the field grow. They do not labor or spin. Yet I tell you that not even Solomon in all his splendor was dressed like one of these. If that is how God clothes the grass of the field, which is here today and tomorrow is thrown into the fire, will he not much more clothe you, O you of little faith? So do not worry, saying, 'What shall we eat?' or 'What shall we drink?' or 'What shall we wear?' For the pagans run after all these things, and your heavenly Father knows that you need them. But seek first his kingdom and his righteousness, and all these things will be given to you as well. Therefore do not worry about tomorrow, for tomorrow will worry about itself. Each day has enough trouble of its own."

– Matthew 6:25-34

worry

I need this reminder constantly. I need to remember I am instructed not to worry. I think it's natural to be on edge about certain things, but lying in bed at night worrying about inane things that are out of my control is taking it a little far. I created this page using a quote from a guest speaker at church and one of my favorite verses. I had never heard it put that way, but it's so true. It really helped me, but I knew if I simply jotted it down on a scratch piece of paper it would get lost at the bottom of my purse. Instead, I decided to make a page about it—one of those great revelations I never want to forget.

this is me year seven as a bulimic. slowly killing myself just to fit in. thank you Lord—for saving me from this... for forgiving me for not holding my past against me. for loving me & helping me learn to love myself. you are an unconditional blessing.

delivered.

DELIVERED

I found these pictures when I was sorting through mounds of photos, and oddly, my first thought wasn't "Oh my gosh, my hair was huge." My first thought was, "That was at the height of my bulimia." This is what a bulimic looks like: so afraid to be myself, having to conform to an ideal I had in my head. I finally realized God had more for me. He didn't want me to destroy the only body I'd been given. It was as though God snapped His fingers and took the desire away. One day, I just decided I wasn't going to do it again, and I never did. It just goes to show that when God is in it, it doesn't have to be hard.

The handwritten journaling on the layout reads:

i have this idea of what a good housewife is ... a perfectly organized home, time + desire to do all those things you never have the time + desire to do, a smoothly running home w/ no glitches. I know I can't measure up to this ideal— but I try anyway and get discouraged when I fail.

I have this idea of what a good Christian looks like... perfectly consistent in time in the Bible + prayer, desires always to be involved in church + ministry, a spiritual walk that runs smoothly w/minus the fierce internal struggles. I know I can't achieve this on my own, but I try anyway + get discouraged when I fail. Lord Jesus, help me to accept your grace in the everyday. Teach me that "your grace is sufficient" for me, that your power is made perfect in (my) weakness." (2 Corinthians 12:9)

Grace
Every Day

by Hanni Baumgardner

Why is it we try to do everything on our own? We forget that God is right there, just waiting for us to ask for His help. Hanni's page explores her own inability to accept God's grace in the everyday. Using a playful design, she has tied together the idea of the perfect housewife and the perfect Christian—and how nobody can ever achieve either one. This layout will be an important reminder to Hanni as she continues to strive to be a good wife and a good Christian woman. We all need those visual reminders every now and then to help us accept all that God has for us, even when we feel like we should be able to do it on our own.

be you. . . it's the best thing you can be.

there is no one like you

k

I see a girl on the verge of growing up. Feeling a bit awkward in her own skin. I see potential. I see imagination. I see beauty... so much beauty even she doesn't see.

Kayla

I see intelligence and talent. I see brains AND beauty. I see you the way God sees you... just as you were meant to be.

what do you see?

I see twelve. The age where girls start to hate themselves. I see someone who is - and always will be - perfect just the way she is.

just be you

you

Most of all, I see myself in this little girl. Still unsure of herself. Not convinced she's got anything to offer. I see sweet with just a little sassy. I see awkward with just enough grace. I see what you're going to become... and I cannot help but be amazed, Kayla... you are more than good enough. You are perfectly you.

YOU ARE ONE OF A KIND

fearfully & wonderfully made...
~ Psalm 139:14

KAYLA

Working with kids has taught me so many lessons. One of these is that I shouldn't have been so hard on myself when I was 12 years old. I learned that from Kayla. She is one of our kids in our church leadership group. In talking with her, I saw me. Age 12. Full of insecurities and worried I'd never fit in. So, I made this layout for Kayla, but also for me. I wanted to tell her what I wish I'd known at her age and to remind myself that I'm not 12 anymore. I don't need to carry those insecurities, because ultimately, the only thing that matters is how God sees me. And like all of His creations, He sees something beautiful.

Don't be afraid to use a photo in your albums just because it doesn't measure up to your normal standards. This photo is technically terrible. I think it was taken with a disposable camera. But it's the only photo I have of August and me. When it comes down to using a less than perfect photo or nothing at all—go with the less than perfect photo every time! The memory is what's really important!

CHALLENGED

I have such vivid memories of August Benassi. An amazingly talented actor, August was a leader on the Bradley Speech Team – a guy who reminded me a lot of my own brother. He was so intimidating – the kind of person who commanded attention. I remember one night on the way home from a tournament, we got into a somewhat religious conversation. He asked me why I believed in God and heaven and why I had faith at all. And you know what? I couldn't answer him. I had no idea at that time why I had such strong convictions – they weren't backed by any substance – it was just the way I'd been raised. Basically, I believed in God because my parents told me to.

I'm older now – and I can easily articulate my beliefs and even use the Bible to back me up... but I'll never forget August and this conversation. The first person who didn't sidestep the issue. He challenged me to explain my beliefs. I didn't take offense to this or look at it as an argument, because from that day to this, I don't carry opinions and beliefs without having the substance to back them up.

Now, I welcome questions about my faith. I know what I believe and why I believe it... but if people like August had never asked me, I wonder... would I have been content to never know the why behind my faith? Would I have been happy to just follow the rules put before me? I'm so thankful I'll never know... thanks, August. Lesson learned.

There was a time in my life when I could articulate what I believed, but I couldn't tell you why I believed it. In college, there was a friend of mine who was the first person to really ask me what turned out to be a life-changing question: Why do you believe in God? In stumbling for an answer, I realized I had no idea why my faith was so important to me. August challenged me to dig into it myself, instead of always accepting what my parents or pastor said was true. I created this layout because I don't want my own kids to simply accept what I say as true. Hopefully, they will dive into their faith and sort through it themselves.

Can you look past your pre-conceived ideas? Can you eliminate the standards? the misconceptions? Can you allow me to be human - fallible - full of mistakes...? Can you accept me - a pastors wife - and know that HE died for my sins too. Can you look past the title & know that i am how & forever will be.

grace

IMPERFECTLY me

FOCUS on FAITH

How do you feel about your faults? Do you hide them from others, or are you open about the areas in which you need a little extra attention? Does it affect your relationship with God, thinking you have to be perfect before you can reach out to Him? You know, He really does love us just as we are—imperfections and all.

IMPERFECTLY ME

Nobody's perfect, are they? And yet, too often we place unrealistic expectations on ourselves and on people in the ministry. We forget that pastors and their wives are human, and they are going to make mistakes. I am well aware of my faults, and while I sometimes beat myself up over them, mostly I want to learn to accept myself as a work in progress. I want to accept others as the same. I want others to accept imperfect me.

Think back on your early church days when everything was new. Perhaps you're new to your religion now. What kinds of object lessons really hit you? What kinds of lessons do you hope you never forget? Write them down. Make pages about them. Make a mini album about them. One of your greatest tools in life is education. Don't re-learn what you already know.

silver dollar lesson

I can distinctly remember learning the importance of tithing. My tooth had just fallen out, and the sweet tooth fairy left me two quarters under my pillow. I was so excited. I suppose somewhere along the way, I'd learned it was good to give money in the offering at church, but I didn't really know why. I took my 50 cents with me to Sunday school and put both coins in the offering, not thinking a thing about it. I must've mentioned my offering to my mom because I can remember her being kind of proud of me for that. Still, I didn't really understand.

The next morning, when I woke up, I discovered something under my pillow. It wasn't a quarter, though - it was bigger than that... when I asked my mom what it was, she told me it was a silver dollar. It was worth one whole dollar! And the tooth fairy must have returned to give me more this time because I'd been so good about giving the first time.

If I'd been really smart, I would've given that silver dollar in the offering the next week, but I didn't. Instead, I learned a lesson far more valuable than any coin. I learned the principle of sowing and reaping. When I give to God what He's asked me for, he gives back to me, double, even triple what I've sacrificed. That principle is still so important in my life today. No matter what, because we are faithful in our giving, God always provides for all of our needs. No matter how low our bank account gets, we will never forget to give our tithe. And I know that because of that, and because of our attitude in doing it, God will never forget to bless us.

silver dollar lesson

or "how i learned to tithe..."

Some lessons we learn as children stick with us for the rest of our lives. For me, this was one of those lessons. As my kids grow, I want to teach them the way I was taught, so they never resent giving money to God. I never questioned it because my dad showed me in such a clear way that in doing so, I am really only benefitting myself. I mean, God is so faithful in giving back to us—He always meets our needs. This is one of those lessons I will never forget, and one that will continue to benefit me throughout my entire life.

One day at church, Sandy shared a vision of a person at a river. He goes in knee-deep, and he's a bit unsteady because of the current. Waist high, and still he stumbles. Chest high, same. He then dives in and the current takes him. He's free. He can swim and move and roll with the current.

How that vision resonated with me. God is my river of life. I know that I should trust Him completely. Yet sometimes, I tread knee-deep in my comfort zone. And I stumble. I hold onto my perceived security, and I'm unsteady. It's so hard to surrender. To give up control. To give Him my all. I know I sometimes hold back parts of my life from him. I'm afraid to give him all of me. I'm afraid of trials he may use to strengthen me. I tell him what I can handle. I tell him he can work on certain parts of my life, but not others. I tell him my children are mine. I tell him my husband is mine. My finances are mine. Yet I know I'm just a steward, a caretaker, fumbling through decisions. Not doing so well on my own. How much lighter my burden would be if I gave them up to him. How much easier my life would be if I surrendered it to him each day. How much better if I learned to swim...

swim *by Nely Fok*

Some of the greatest lessons of life are lessons we are in the process of learning. Nely uses a beautiful analogy to convey her thoughts on turning the important aspects of her life over to God. Acting almost as a reminder to herself, this layout is a confession of the difficulty she is having with the idea. With a simple design and a striking photo, Nely has created a page that will speak to generations, allowing her children to know she didn't have everything figured out; she was still relying on God for the answers.

Consider a different approach to your faith-based pages. Why not add a little laughter? We can either have a little chuckle at our own shortcomings—those lessons we seem to be unable to learn—or we can beat ourselves up over them. I have a feeling God would want us to choose the laughter! Besides, humor is a wonderful addition to any scrapbook!

Letting Go...

by Letting God

Givin' your troubles
to the Lord,
should be an easy thang...

But when I try,
they come back at me...
just like a boomerang.

I squint my eyes,
and grit my teeth,
and then I start to pray...

"Oh Lord above,
just hear my plea
and take this mess away!"

But, there I stand
waist deep in muck...
(getting deeper all the time).

"Where are you, Lord?"
I yell out loud,
as my troubles continue to climb.

Then low and behold,
I realize,
(just as I start to lose hope)...

I keep tugging and tugging
and getting nowhere...
'cuz it's me at both ends of the rope.

I've never let go,
Thus, never let God
do what He does best...

So I finally let go,
(of that stupid old rope)
and now, I truly am blessed.

~Torrey Scott

LETTING GO

by Jodi Amidei

"Cast all your cares on Him for He cares for you..." It's easy to quote scripture, but it's terribly difficult to do what scripture tells us to do. Jodi took a humorous approach in creating a page about a hard-learned lesson, allowing her to remember not to take life so seriously. She edited the photo to create a mirror image reflecting the only person she's in a tug of war with—herself.

He WiLL always CaRRy yoU

Just as your daddy *carries* you when you are tired you are learning a valuable lesson in knowing that your *Heavenly Father* will *always* do the same! I know you will face some struggles in your lifetime; no matter how much I pray for that to never happen; but you have a   with the *One that will carry* you when you are too weak to walk; too tired to lift your head; *no matter what* the circumstance; He will be there carrying you. *Never forget* that my sweet girl! You have a   both on earth and up in Heaven *watching over you* all the time!

He will cover you with his feathers, and under his wings you will find refuge; his faithfulness will be your shield and rampart. Psalms 91:4 (niv)

HE WILL CARRY YOU *by Heather Preckel*

Heather's layout is a powerful reminder to her daughter that just as her earthly father carries and protects her, her Heavenly Father will do the same. Using an enlarged photo of Kiersten on her daddy's shoulders, Heather is able to convey the idea perfectly. Accented with a promise from the book of Psalms, Kiersten will never have to wonder if God loves her and will protect her. To be certain, He will.

contributors

Ruth Akers

Ruth has been scrapbooking for about five years now, though she's always kept decorated journals for her photos. Her favorite thing about this hobby is that there are no rules, and it's her unique style that sets her apart from the crowd. Ruth has been a part of the Church of Jesus Christ of Latter-Day Saints for her entire life, and considers her faith to be the reason she is here on this earth. She explains that she scrapbooks because of what her faith has taught her: to show her kids she loves them and to swerve when life throws you curveballs. For Ruth, scrapbooking her faith comes naturally because her faith is embedded in all she does. She says she doesn't want to simply be remembered as a wife or a mother—she wants future generations to know what she believes and why she believes it. She and her husband Mike have three kids with their fourth on the way.

Jodi Amidei

A professional scrapbooker for over seven years, Jodi was an original Memory Makers Master but left her title behind to become an editor on staff. She is a non-denominational Christian who believes her faith gives her something to believe and trust in, and also feels it is of the utmost importance to share this aspect of her life with future generations. There are many aspects of scrapbooking that appeal to this artist, but it is the creative process that keeps her coming back for more. Jodi says it fulfills the instinctive need she has to be artistic. She lives in Colorado with her husband Tom and their ten-year-old daughter, Haley.

Hanni Baumgardner

Hanni began scrapbooking almost seven years ago, and she hasn't looked back since! A self-professed homebody, Hanni loves cooking, playing the piano and fussing around in the garden with her flowers. Hanni has been a follower of Jesus Christ her entire life and continues to live out her beliefs day by day. However, her selfless nature doesn't keep her from hiding chocolate in numerous places throughout her house! According to Hanni, creativity is a gift from God, so she likes her scrapbooking to honor Him by using her gift for her glory. Sometimes that simply means enjoying the process! Hanni lives in Indiana with her wonderful husband Doug and their shih tzu, Miyagi.

Amber Clark

Raised in a Brethren church, Amber grew up with a strong sense of all things spiritual, something she continues to hold onto today. While she hasn't been to church in about five years, Amber says it is still very much a part of who she is. "I just celebrate my religion in a different way now," she explains. She has been scrapbooking about five years now, and loves telling stories through her art. Scrapbooking her faith is important to Amber because she wants her son to know her views, why she does what she does and feels how she feels. Scrapbooking also brings perspective to her life. Amber lives in Ohio with her fiance and her son.

Nely Fok

Nely loves everything about scrapbooking. Since discovering this hobby five years ago, she has grown to love it all, from the photography, to sharing her stories, to passing down traditions, to every girl's favorite past time, shopping! Nely has been a Christian since she was five years old, and credits her faith with her ability to accept herself just as she is, in spite of being a perfectionist who wants to get everything right. Knowing that God's grace is sufficient gets her through, even when she messes up. Nely feels it's important to scrapbook her faith to record all that God has done for her to remind her just how good God is. Nely and her husband live in San Diego, California, with their two daughters.

Deb Perry

Deb has been scrapbooking for almost four years and has a number of accomplishments to her credit. Her work has been featured in a variety of publications, and she has been a finalist in both the Memory Makers Masters Contest and the Creating Keepsakes Hall of Fame. She is also on a number of manufacturer design teams. Deb has been a born again Christian since she accepted Christ at the age of five. She and her husband currently serve on the worship team at their Baptist Church and are involved in a number of other ministries as well. When asked why she feels it's important to scrapbook your faith, Deb replies, "If God permeates all of my life, how could I not let my faith shine through this work as well? I want to not only leave my family a legacy of memories and photos but a recorded spiritual legacy as well." Deb, her husband and three children make their home in Newport News, Virginia.

Heather Preckel

A widely published scrapbooker who has been scrapbooking for eight years, Heather loves the creative outlet this hobby gives her, something she hasn't been able to find anywhere else. Heather became a born again Christian when she was 16 and continues to keep her faith at the center of her life. She says her heart longs to serve Jesus Christ, following after Him no matter what she is doing. It is her hope that people will look at her pages and see that she was real; that she shared her heart as best she could, writing words and telling stories that are influenced by Him. To Heather, it is important to leave a legacy of faith behind for others to see and follow. Heather and her husband, Steve, live in North Carolina with their daughter Kiersten.

Brenda-Mae Teo

Brenda-Mae is a born again Christian living overseas. She is a widely published scrapbooker who views this hobby as a vital part of her daily life. With her family as her inspiration and her love of ribbon, paper, magazines and idea books, not to mention the computer, the camera and the sewing machine to guide her, Brenda-Mae always seems to find a unique spin in every page she creates. Throughout her life, she strives to know God more and to discover his daily purposes for her and for her family. Brenda lives in Singapore with her husband and two sons.

Chapter One
I BELIEVE

I BELIEVE {10}
Digital patterned paper, frame (Two Peas in a Bucket); crosses (Internet downloads); Copperplate Gothic Light font (Microsoft); Iris font (Internet download); Kreider font (Chatterbox)

THE TINIEST PRAYERS {11}
Digital patterned paper (Two Peas in a Bucket); stitches (Shabby Shoppe); inked edges (Digital Design Essentials); Clarendon font (Internet download)

SPEAK LIFE {12}
Digital distressing brush, flower brush, frame (Two Peas in a Bucket); Century Gothic font (Microsoft); Freestyle Script fonts (Internet download)

HEARTBREAK {13}
Digital patterned paper, frame (Two Peas in a Bucket); brads (Digital Design Essentials); LauraMc, Stereofidelic fonts (Internet downloads); Mrs. Morgan font (Chatterbox)

INTO MY HEART {14}
Patterned paper, photo corners (Scenic Route Paper Co.); chipboard letters (Heidi Swapp); chipboard heart (Pressed Petals); buttons (Autumn Leaves); stamp (FontWerks); pigment ink; embroidery floss; pen; cardstock

JESUS, HEAL MY BUMPS {15}
Patterned paper (Chatterbox); chipboard letters (Making Memories); metal letters (American Crafts); plastic letters (Paper Studio); rub-ons letters (Doodlebug Designs); buttons (Autumn Leaves); embroidery floss; rickrack (Wrights); cardstock; Arial font (Microsoft)

SHE SEES ANGELS {16}
Patterned paper (Autumn Leaves); rub-ons (7 Gypsies, Arctic Frog, BasicGrey, Creative Imaginations); flowers (Prima); brads (Making Memories); dye ink; pen; cardstock

JUST LOOK RIGHT HERE {17}
Patterned paper (7 Gypsies, BasicGrey, Chatterbox); rub-ons (Chatterbox, Memories Complete); stickers (7 Gypsies, Autumn Leaves, Chatterbox, Doodlebug Designs, EK Success); dye ink; corner rounder; marker

IN CHRIST ALONE {18}
Patterned paper, magnets, ribbon (BasicGrey); rub-ons (BasicGrey, Royal & Langnickel); buttons (source unknown); circle punch; acrylic paint; marker; pen; cardstock

CREATIVE GENIUS {19}
Digital patterned paper, borders, frames (Two Peas in a Bucket); AL Sandra, Dekka Dense JL, Eurostile fonts (Internet downloads)

STILL SMALL VOICE {20}
Patterned paper, coaster letters, paper tabs, rub-ons (Imagination Project); ribbons (Autumn Leaves, May Arts, Michaels); rickrack (Wrights); buttons (Autumn Leaves); embroidery floss; kraft paper; staples; dye ink; cardstock

A SENSE OF HUMOR {21}
Patterned paper, letter stickers (Arctic Frog); buttons (Junkitz); embroidery floss; pigment ink; acrylic paint; kraft cardstock; Blue Highway font (Internet download); Century Gothic font (Microsoft)

WHY CHURCH? {22}
Digital patterned paper (Digital Design Essentials, Two Peas in a Bucket); frame, tree brush (Two Peas in a Bucket); brads (Digital Design Essentials); 10 Minutes, Agent Orange fonts (Internet download)

I BELIEVE {23}
Image editing software (Adobe); Adler font (Internet download); Arial, Times New Roman fonts (Microsoft)

I AM NOT ASHAMED {24}
Digital patterned paper (MoJackson, ScrapArtist); brads, decorative tape, staples, tag (ScrapArtist); frame, design elements (MoJackson); AL Messenger, Resurrection fonts (Internet download)

FAITH KIDS {25}
Digital paper, brush, overlay (Two Peas in a Bucket); Courier New font (Microsoft)

Chapter Two
PRAYERS AND MEDITATIONS

WHEN YOU CALL ON JESUS {28}
Digital patterned paper (Spaceraven); circle stamps (Two Peas in a Bucket); doodle lines, handwriting (Wacom tablet); song lyrics (Nicole Mullen)

THE LITTLE THINGS {29}
Cardstock; letter stickers (Chatterbox); rub-ons (BasicGrey, Creative Imaginations); fuzzy rub-on (Heidi Swapp); pen; cardstock

BLESSING LINDSAE {30}
Patterned paper (A2Z Essentials); chipboard letters, rub-ons (Heidi Grace Designs); flower coaster (Imagination Project); digital frame (ScrapArtist); dye ink; pen; cardstock; Billboard font (Two Peas in a Bucket)

 I PRAY {31}
Patterned paper (Scrapworks); letter and word stickers (Heidi Swapp); circle punch; buttons (Junkitz); embroidery floss; rickrack; dye ink; marker; cardstock; Perpetua font (Microsoft)

 FEAR NOT {32}
Patterned paper (Chatterbox); rub-ons (7 Gypsies, Chatterbox); distress ink (Ranger); embroidery floss; cardstock; Bickley Script font (Internet download); Century Gothic, Copperplate Gothic fonts (Microsoft)

 INVISIBLE {33}
Patterned paper (7 Gypsies, Chatterbox, Creative Imaginations); plastic letters (Heidi Swapp); buttons, file folder (Autumn Leaves); flower and letter stickers (Making Memories); brad; decorative tape, photo turn (7 Gypsies); stamps (Autumn Leaves, My Sentiments Exactly); dye ink; ribbon (May Arts); decorative clip (EK Success); pen; cardstock

 PRAISE YOU, LORD {34}
Cardstock; brads (Queen & Co.); die-cut letters (Provo Craft); rub-on, square accent (source unknown)

 REFUGE {35}
Patterned paper (Chatterbox); chipboard letters and stars (Heidi Swapp); chipboard tile (Scenic Route Paper Co.); rub-ons (Imagination Project); embroidery floss; pigment ink; acrylic paint; corner rounder; cardstock; Century Gothic font (Microsoft)

 A MOTHER'S PRAYER {36}
Patterned paper, photo corner, ribbon (Chatterbox); button (Junkitz); embroidery floss; pen; cardstock

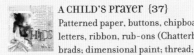 **A CHILD'S PRAYER {37}**
Patterned paper, buttons, chipboard letters, ribbon, rub-ons (Chatterbox); brads; dimensional paint; thread; mesh; cardstock

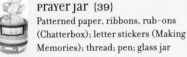 **IN THIS STORM {38}**
Patterned paper (BasicGrey); letter stickers (Jo-Ann Stores); chipboard letters (source unknown); brads; thread; cardboard; newspaper; dye ink; dimensional paint; pen; cardstock; Grand Keymong font (Internet download); lyrics (Casting Crowns)

 REST IN HIM PRAYER JAR {39}
Patterned paper, ribbons, rub-ons (Chatterbox); letter stickers (Making Memories); thread; pen; glass jar

 LAMENTATIONS {40}
Patterned paper (Anna Griffin, Autumn Leaves, My Mind's Eye); chipboard letters (Heidi Swapp); ribbon (May Arts); decorative tape, index tab, rub-ons (7 Gypsies); stamps (My Sentiments Exactly, Savvy Stamps); dye ink; buttons, decorative brad (Autumn Leaves); flower, small brad, trim (Making Memories); lace (source unknown); adhesive foam; cardstock; AL Updated Classic font (Internet download)

 YOU MAKE GOD SMILE {41}
Patterned paper, brad, rub-on (Chatterbox); acrylic paint; letter stickers (Making Memories); plastic letters (Paper Studio); ghost word (Heidi Swapp); ribbon (source unknown); embroidery floss; dimensional paint; sandpaper; cardboard

 BELOVED {42}
Patterned paper, photo corners (Chatterbox); chipboard letters (Heidi Swapp); circle cutter; dye ink; pen; cardstock; Block font (Two Peas in a Bucket)

RAW {43}
Patterned paper (American Crafts, KI Memories); chipboard letters (Heidi Swapp); metal letters (American Crafts); plastic letters (Paper Studio); buttons (Junkitz); embroidery floss; rickrack; corner rounder; pen; cardstock

Chapter Three
PEOPLE WHO INSPIRE

 YOUR PASSION {46}
Patterned paper (Creative Imaginations, Scenic Route Paper Co.); plastic letters (Paper Studio); fabric (Junkitz); buttons, canvas ribbon (Autumn Leaves); embroidery floss; chipboard sticker (Creative Imaginations); journaling square (Making Memories); pen; cardstock

 GOD'S GIFTS {47}
Digital brushes and frames (Two Peas in a Bucket); splotch accent (Designer Digitals); Garbageschrift font (Internet download); Gill Sans MT font (Microsoft); Isabella font (Chatterbox)

 ADVOCATE {48}
Cardstock; flowers (Prima); brads; letter stickers (American Crafts); Arial font (Microsoft)

 ANOINTED {49}
Patterned paper (Arctic Frog, KI Memories); letter stickers (American Crafts); flower stickers (KI Memories); notebook paper; pigment ink; pen; cardstock

 BE QUIET FIRST {50}
Patterned paper, flowers (Chatterbox); thread; cardstock; Black Jack title font (Internet download)

 INSPIRED BY YOU {51}
Digital papers and frame (Two Peas in a Bucket); stitches (Shabby Shoppe); tab (Digital Design Essentials); Arial font (Microsoft); Corabel font (Internet download)

BEAUTIFUL FEET {52}
Digital papers (Mo Jackson, ScrapArtist); buttons, flowers, ribbons, stitches (Mo Jackson); letters (ScrapArtist); Garamouche, Modern Type fonts (Internet downloads)

 U JUST MEAN IT {53}
Patterned paper, letters, rub-ons, stickers, decorative accents (Chatterbox); embroidery floss; pen; cardstock

 YOU MADE ME SEE {54}
Patterned paper (Scenic Route Paper Co.); chipboard letters (Pressed Petals); letter stickers (EK Success); brads, photo corner (Chatterbox); rub-ons (Cherry Arte); stamps (7 Gypsies, Savvy Stamps); pigment ink; ribbon (May Arts); cardstock; Century Gothic font (Microsoft)

 IN AWE OF YOU {55}
Digital papers (Shabby Shoppe, Two Peas in a Bucket); stitches (Shabby Shoppe); distressing brush, frame, overlay (Two Peas in a Bucket); brads (Digital Design Essentials); Century Gothic font (Microsoft)

 DELIVERED INTO DESTINY {56}
Patterned paper, tags (BasicGrey); letter stickers (Arctic Frog); chipboard letters (Pressed Petals); labels (Dymo); brad (Chatterbox); corner rounder; distress ink (Ranger); pen; cardstock

 TAUGHT BY EXAMPLE {58}
Patterned paper (My Mind's Eye); chipboard letters (Wal-Mart); rub-ons (Chatterbox); circle cutter; chipboard accents; adhesive foam; sandpaper

THANKS {59}
Patterned paper, chipboard letters, rub-ons (Cactus Pink); ribbon (Chatterbox); acrylic paint; button (Autumn Leaves); pen; cardstock

 PASTOR'S WIVES {60}
Patterned paper (Provo Craft); chipboard letters (Heidi Swapp, Li'l Davis Designs, Making Memories); plastic letters (Making Memories); flowers (Prima); brads; ribbons (Chatterbox, Making Memories, Michaels); buttons (Junkitz); embroidery floss; acrylic paint; dye ink; pen; cardstock

 FREE SPIRIT {61}
Patterned paper, chipboard letters (All My Memories); chipboard accent (Maya Road); brad; glitter; crystal lacquer (Ranger); adhesive foam; pen; cardstock

Chapter Four
TRADITIONS AND SYMBOLS

 COME HOME {64}
Patterned paper, letter stickers (Chatterbox); chipboard letters (Pressed Petals); buttons (Autumn Leaves); embroidery floss; distress ink (Ranger); cardstock; Vivaldi font (Internet download)

 LAY ME DOWN TO SLEEP {65}
Patterned paper (Chatterbox, Scenic Route Paper Co.); letter stickers (EK Success); rub-ons (KI Memories); dye ink; marker; Arial font (Microsoft); Diesel font (Internet download)

 BLESSING DAY {66}
Patterned paper (Three Bugs in a Rug); letter stickers (American Crafts, Doodlebug Designs); conchos (Scrapworks); brads (Bazzill); thread; dye ink; dimensional paint; hole punches; cardstock

 EGGSTRAVAGANZA {67}
Patterned paper (BasicGrey); rub-on letters (Imagination Project); conchos (Scrapworks);

buttons (Making Memories); embroidery floss; pink clip (source unknown); pigment ink; corner rounder; Courier New font (Microsoft)

 MAKING STORIES {68}
Patterned paper, rub-ons (Chatterbox); square letter stickers (Wal-Mart); sticker accents (7 Gypsies); marker; pen

 CTR {69}
Cardstock; acrylic paint; dimensional paint; letter accents (Doodlebug Designs, Heidi Swapp); bookplates (Jo-Ann Stores); conchos (Scrapworks); brads; thread; dye ink; pen

 THE POWER OF PRAYER {70}
Patterned paper, letter stickers (BasicGrey); fabric (Junkitz); buttons (Autumn Leaves); embroidery floss; distress ink (Ranger); cardstock; Century Gothic font (Microsoft)

 ANYTHING BUT TRADITIONAL {71}
Patterned paper (Scenic Route Paper Co.); chipboard letters (Li'l Davis Designs); ribbon (May Arts); embroidery floss; staples; dye ink; pen; transparency; cardstock; Times New Roman font (Microsoft)

SURRENDER {72}
Patterned paper, sticker trim (Scrapworks); buttons (source unknown); embroidery floss; pigment ink; circle cutter; cardstock; Britannic Bold, Century Gothic fonts (Microsoft)

HOME CHURCH {73}
Patterned paper (A2Z Essentials); ribbon (Offray); rickrack (May Arts); brads; adhesive foam; dye ink; pen; cardstock; P22 Garamouche font (Internet download)

AT THE CROSS {74}
Patterned paper (Chatterbox); foam stamps, rhinestones (Making Memories); acrylic paint; flowers (Chatterbox, Prima); ribbon (Offray); adhesive foam; pen; cardstock

SONG OF MY SOUL {75}
Patterned paper (K & Company); die-cut letters (QuicKutz); rub-ons (Chatterbox); adhesive foam; cardstock

SAFE FLIGHT {76}
Patterned paper, sticker accents, tags (Scrapworks); letter stickers (source unknown); pen; cardstock; Century Gothic font (Microsoft)

SOMEONE'S WATCHING OVER ME {77}
Patterned paper (Paper Studio); die-cut letters (QuicKutz); letter stamps (Limited Edition); dye ink; ribbon (Michaels); brads; paper flower (Chatterbox); metal bookplate (Nunn Designs); adhesive foam; pen; cardstock

NAMED BY GOD {78}
Patterned paper, letter stickers, tags (BasicGrey); chipboard stars (Heidi Swapp); acrylic paint; brads (Chatterbox); corner rounder; cardstock; Arial font (Microsoft)

TATTOO OF FAITH {79}
Patterned paper, rub-ons (Chatterbox); adhesive foam; corner rounder; AL Sandra font (Internet download); Century Gothic font (Microsoft)

Chapter Five
BLESSINGS

MIRACULOUS {82}
Patterned paper (KI Memories); rub-ons (Chatterbox, KI Memories); distress ink (Ranger); corner rounder; Velcro; cardstock; Arial font (Microsoft); Bickley Script title font (Internet download)

TIME TO PAUSE {83}
Patterned paper, photo corner (Chatterbox); chipboard letters (Li'l Davis Designs); letter stickers (BasicGrey); ribbon, rickrack (American Crafts, May Arts); buttons (Autumn Leaves, Making Memories); photo turn, rub-on (7 Gypsies); brads (Making Memories); staples; dye ink; cardstock; Courier New font (Microsoft)

BLESSING {84}
Patterned paper, rub-on trim (Chatterbox); circle punch; cardstock; Iphegenia title font (Internet download)

STORY OF GOD'S HOME {85}
Patterned paper (7 Gypsies, Chatterbox); brads, letter stickers, photo corners (Chatterbox); rub-ons (7 Gypsies, Chatterbox, Imagination Project); photo turns (7 Gypsies); corner rounder; pens

HE KNEW {86}
Patterned paper, photo corners, rub-ons (Chatterbox); letter stickers (Scrapworks); distress ink (Ranger); First Home font (Internet download)

LAND OF THE FREE {87}
Digital patterned paper (Digital Design Essentials); stitches (Shabby Shoppe); Georgia font (Microsoft)

SHARPEN {88}
Patterned paper (Scenic Route Paper Co.); letter stickers (American Crafts); circle punch; distress ink (Ranger); embroidery floss; Velcro; pen; cardstock; Arial font (Microsoft)

SO THANKFUL {89}
Patterned paper (Scenic Route Paper Co.); letter stamps (Fontwerks); pigment ink; photo turns (7 Gypsies); buttons (Autumn Leaves); embroidery floss; bookplate (Junkitz); die-cut photo corner; sandpaper; pen; cardstock

I FIT {90}
Digital patterned paper, floral edge, stitching (Shabby Shoppe); puzzle overlay (Digital Scrapbook Place); Century Gothic font (Microsoft); Corabel font (Internet download)

MAMA TO A MONKEY {91}
Patterned paper (Autumn Leaves, KI Memories); fabric tabs, rubber letters (Scrapworks); rub-on letters (Li'l Davis Designs); brads (Chatterbox); corner rounder; pen; cardstock

ONE BABY, FIVE MIRACLES {92}
Patterned paper (source unknown); letter stickers (American Crafts); rub-on words (Deja Views); rub-on flowers (KI Memories); ribbon (Chatterbox); pigment ink; tag; pen; cardstock

GROWN UP {94}
Digital patterned paper (Shabby Shoppe); overlay, brush (Two Peas in a Bucket); Century Gothic font (Microsoft); Generic title font (Internet download)

HE SAW THE FUTURE {95}
Patterned paper (Autumn Leaves, Chatterbox); square letter stickers (Wal-Mart); accent stickers (7 Gypsies, EK Success); photo corners, rub-on (Chatterbox); marker; Impact font (Microsoft)

DOUBLE BLESSING {96}
Patterned paper (BasicGrey); chipboard letters (Heidi Swapp); rub-on stitches (Doodlebug Designs); die-cut flower punch (Hot Off the Press); brads; dye ink; acrylic paint; pen; cardstock

DEAR GOD {97}
Patterned paper (7 Gypsies, Chatterbox); chipboard letters (source unknown); sticker details (7 Gypsies, American Crafts, EK Success, Heidi Swapp); rub-on (Chatterbox); circle cutter; marker

KEPT {98}
Cardstock; plastic letters (Paper Studio); chipboard accent (Maya Road); acrylic paint; corner rounder; pen; cardstock; Courier New font (Microsoft); journaling verse (Debra Arnott)

BEFORE AND AFTER BLESSING {99}
Digital patterned paper, brushes, frames (Two Peas in a Bucket); photo turns (Shabby Shoppe); CafeCoco font (Internet download); Isabella font (Chatterbox)

Chapter Six
LESSONS OF FAITH

NEVER COMPROMISE {102}
Digital patterned paper (Two Peas in a Bucket); stitches (Shabby Shoppe); eyelet trim (Oscraps); CafeCoco, Dekka Dense JL fonts (Internet download)

TRUST {103}
Patterned paper, buttons, round letter stickers, thread flourish (Autumn Leaves); chipboard letters (Li'l Davis Designs); chipboard arrow (KI Memories); rub-ons (Fontwerks); ribbon, rickrack (American Crafts, May Arts); lace (source unknown); thread; pen; cardstock

YES, JESUS LOVES YOU {104}
Patterned paper (KI Memories, Scenic Route Paper Co.); chipboard letters and shapes (Heidi Swapp, Pressed Petals); decorative tape (Heidi Swapp); envelope; notebook paper; pen; cardstock; Mom's Typewriter font (Internet download)

MIXED NUTS {105}
Patterned paper (American Crafts, Around the Block); letter stickers, buttons (source unknown); conchos (Scrapworks); brads; dimensional paint; thread; cardstock

A LETTER TO MYSELF {106}
Patterned paper, chipboard stickers (Creative Imaginations); chipboard letters (Heidi Swapp); ribbon (Autumn Leaves, Making Memories); buttons (Autumn Leaves); rub-ons (Imagination Project); dimensional paint; embroidery floss; envelope (Bazzill); fabric (Junkitz); metal clips (office supply store); pigment ink; sewing pin; pen; cardstock

WORRY {108}
Patterned paper (Imagination Project); brad, flower, letter stickers (Chatterbox); corner rounder; cardstock; Arial font (Microsoft)

DELIVERED {109}
Patterned paper, photo corners, ribbon (KI Memories); letter stickers (Doodlebug Designs); embroidery floss; pen

GRACE EVERY DAY {110}
Patterned paper, chipboard photo turn, letter stickers (BasicGrey); brad; acrylic paint; thread; pen

KAYLA {111}
Patterned paper (A2Z Essentials); rub-ons, stickers, tags (Creative Imaginations); brads (Making Memories); button; embroidery floss; dye ink; pen; cardstock; Arial font (Microsoft); Flourishes, Mrs. Morgan fonts (Chatterbox)

CHALLENGED {112}
Patterned paper (KI Memories, Scenic Route Paper Co.); letter stickers, chipboard arrows (KI Memories); photo turns (7 Gypsies); brads; cardstock; Arial font (Microsoft)

IMPERFECTLY ME {113}
Cardstock; chipboard letters and stars, plastic letters (Heidi Swapp); letter stickers (American Crafts); flowers, cut-outs (KI Memories); rhinestones (Making Memories); ribbon (Arctic Frog); buttons (Autumn Leaves); embroidery floss; sandpaper; pen

SILVER DOLLAR LESSON {114}
Patterned paper (Scrapworks); letter stickers (Arctic Frog); brads, flowers (Chatterbox); embroidery floss; ribbon (May Arts); corner rounder; pen; cardstock; Garamond font (Microsoft)

SWIM {115}
Patterned paper (Scenic Route Paper Co.); buttons (Autumn Leaves); sticker trim (Deluxe Designs); thread; cardstock; Staccato 225 title font (Internet download)

LETTING GO {116}
Photographer: Torrey Scott
Patterned paper (My Mind's Eye); photo turns (Queen & Co.); brads; adhesive foam; image editing software (Adobe); textured cardstock

HE WILL ALWAYS CARRY YOU {117}
Patterned paper, rub-on accents (BasicGrey); chipboard letters (Heidi Swapp); ribbon (May Arts); buttons (Junkitz); word flashcard (7 Gypsies); dye ink; pen; cardstock; Typewriter font (Internet download)

source guide

The following companies manufacture products featured in this book. Please check your local retailers to find these materials, or go to a company's Web site for the latest product. In addition, we have made every attempt to properly credit the items mentioned in this book. We apologize to any company that we have listed incorrectly, and we would appreciate hearing from you.

7 Gypsies
(877) 749-7797
www.sevengypsies.com

A2Z Essentials
(419) 663-2869
www.geta2z.com

Adobe Systems Incorporated
(800) 833-6687
www.adobe.com

All My Memories
(888) 553-1998
www.allmymemories.com

American Crafts
(801) 226-0747
www.americancrafts.com

Anna Griffin, Inc.
(888) 817-8170
www.annagriffin.com

Arctic Frog
(479) 636-3764
www.arcticfrog.com

Around The Block
(801) 593-1946
www.aroundtheblockproducts.com

Autumn Leaves
(800) 588-6707
www.autumnleaves.com

BasicGrey
(801) 544-1116
www.basicgrey.com

Bazzill Basics Paper
(480) 558-8557
www.bazzillbasics.com

Berwick Offray, LLC
(800) 344-5533
www.offray.com

Cactus Pink
(866) 798-2446
www.cactuspink.com

Casting Crowns
www.castingcrowns.com

Chatterbox, Inc.
(888) 416-6260
www.chatterboxinc.com

Cherry Arte
(212) 465-3495
www.cherryarte.com

Creative Imaginations
(800) 942-6487
www.cigift.com

Crossed Paths
(972) 393-3755
www.crossedpaths.net

Dèjá Views
(800) 243-8419
www.dejaviews.com

Deluxe Designs
(480) 497-9005
www.deluxecuts.com

Designer Digitals
www.designerdigitals.com

Digital Design Essentials
www.digitaldesignessentials.com

Digital Scrapbook Place, The
(866) 396-6906
www.digitalscrapbookplace.com

DMC Corp.
(973) 589-0606
www.dmc-usa.com

Doodlebug Design Inc.
(877) 800-9190
www.doodlebug.ws

Dymo
(800) 426-7827
www.dymo.com

EK Success, Ltd.
(800) 524-1349
www.eksuccess.com

Fancy Pants Designs, LLC
(801) 779-3212
www.fancypantsdesigns.com

FontWerks
(604) 942-3105
www.fontwerks.com

Heidi Grace Designs, Inc.
(866) 348-5661
www.heidigrace.com

Heidi Swapp/Advantus Corporation
(904) 482-0092
www.heidiswapp.com

Hot Off The Press, Inc.
(800) 227-9595
www.b2b.hotp.com

Imagination Project, Inc.
(888) 477-6532
www.imaginationproject.com

Jo-Ann Stores
www.joann.com

Junkitz
(732) 792-1108
www.junkitz.com

K & Company
(888) 244-2083
www.kandcompany.com

KI Memories
(972) 243-5595
www.kimemories.com

Li'l Davis Designs
(480) 223-0080
www.lildavisdesigns.com

Limited Edition Rubberstamps
(800) 229-1019
www.limitededitionrs.com

Making Memories
(801) 294-0430
www.makingmemories.com

May Arts
(800) 442-3950
www.mayarts.com

Maya Road, LLC
(214) 488-3279
www.mayaroad.com

Memories Complete, LLC
(866) 966-6365
www.memoriescomplete.com

Michaels Arts & Crafts
(800) 642-4235
www.michaels.com

Microsoft Corporation
www.microsoft.com

Mo Jackson
www.mojackson.com

My Mind's Eye, Inc.
(866) 989-0320
www.mymindseye.com

My Sentiments Exactly
(719) 260-6001
www.sentiments.com

Nicole Mullen
www.nicolecmullen.com

Nunn Design
(800) 761-3557
www.nunndesign.com

Offray - see Berwick Offray, LLC

Oscraps.
www.oscraps.com

Paper Studio
(480) 557-5700
www.paperstudio.com

Pressed Petals
(800) 748-4656
www.pressedpetals.com

Prima Marketing, Inc.
(909) 627-5532
www.primamarketinginc.com

Provo Craft
(800) 937-7686
www.provocraft.com

Queen & Co.
(858) 613-7858
www.queenandcompany.com

QuicKutz, Inc.
(888) 702-1146
www.quickutz.com

Ranger Industries, Inc.
(800) 244-2211
www.rangerink.com

Royal & Langnickel/Royal Brush Mfg.
(800) 247-2211
www.royalbrush.com

Savvy Stamps
(866) 447-2889
www.savvystamps.com

Scenic Route Paper Co.
(801) 225-5754
www.scenicroutepaper.com

Scrap Girls
(866) 598-3444
www.scrapgirls.com

ScrapArtist
www.scrapartist.com

Scrapworks, LLC / As You Wish Products, LLC
(801) 363-1010
www.scrapworks.com

Shabby Princess
www.shabbyprincess.com

Shabby Shoppe, The
www.theshabbyshoppe.com

Spaceraven
www.spaceraven.net

Stampabilities
(800) 888-0321
www.stampabilities.com

Therm O Web, Inc.
(800) 323-0799
www.thermoweb.com

Three Bugs in a Rug, LLC
(801) 804-6657
www.threebugsinarug.com

Tsukineko, Inc.
(800) 769-6633
www.tsukineko.com

Two Peas in a Bucket
(888) 896-7327
www.twopeasinabucket.com

Wacom Technology
(800) 922-9348
www.wacom.com

Wal-Mart Stores, Inc.
www.walmart.com

Wrights Ribbon Accents
(877) 597-4448
www.wrights.com

index

Find more inspiration in these great books from Memory Makers.

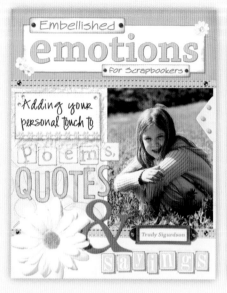

Embellished Emotions

Learn from scrapbook artist
Trudy Sigurdson how to begin
a journey into capturing emotion
on scrapbook pages through the
use of poems, quotes and sayings.

ISBN-13: 978-1-892127-84-6
ISBN-10: 1-892127-84-9

paperback
112 pages

Z0023

Scrapbook Designer's Workbook

Join author Kari Hansen as she
takes the fear out of understanding and using design principles to
create fabulous scrapbook layouts.

ISBN-13: 978-1-892127-95-2
ISBN-10: 1-892127-95-4

hardcover with enclosed spiral
128 pages

Z0533

What About the Words?

Journaling on your scrapbook
layouts is easy with the advice,
examples and inspirations
found here.

ISBN-13: 978-1-892127-77-8
ISBN-10: 1-892127-77-6

paperback
128 pages

Z0017

These books and other fine Memory Makers titles are available at your local craft or scrapbook store,
bookstore or from online suppliers, including www.memorymakersmagazine.com.